ALGO TRADING
2022

Techniques and Algorithmic Trading Systems for Successful Investing

Table of Contents

DISCLAIMER

Individual performance depends upon each student's unique skills, time commitment and effort. Results may not be typical and individual results will vary.

codes to get these bonuses:

- **Code Packages** – Tradestation code for many of the studies in this book

- **"6 Nifty Extras"**–not entries, not exits, but instead useful code snippets for Tradestation you can use for algo trading

- **Free Mini S&P Algo Strategy** with fully disclosed code

- **Invitations to free trading webinars** I offer, free articles I write and more!

INTRODUCTION

Note before you start: If you are reading the black and white paperback version, due to printing variations and size constraints, sometimes the graphics might be difficult to read.

If you are new to algo trading, or don't even know what algorithmic trading is, just stop reading now. This book is not for you – yet. Maybe try my "Intro To Algo Trading" book instead.

Also, if you are a seasoned expert algo trader, and you are perfectly happy with your risk adjusted performance, you might not find a whole lot of new information in this book. It might be better just to keep doing what you are doing.

However, if you somewhere between beginner and expert, like most of us are, you are in luck. This book is really for the majority of traders stuck somewhere in the middle – experienced algo traders just looking for ideas and tips to improve their trading. That is exactly the type of trader this book is for.

In this book, I reveal a lot of the research I've done in the past year or two – research I have used to improve my algo trading. By using the results of my work, you can use my findings to improve your strategies, too.

Note that I do not discuss position sizing, psychology, portfolio management or other important topics here. Why not? Although I definitely think they are important, my objective in this book is to help traders get better at their algo trading system development. Psychology is VERY important, but will not help you if you have terrible algo strategies!

For me, successful trading starts with edges that you exploit via your algo trading systems.

Perhaps an analogy will help.

If you play blackjack in a casino, in the long run you will lose – pretty much guaranteed. This is regardless of your position sizing, your money management approach, your psychology and discipline (even wisely avoiding the mind numbing free alcoholic drinks!).

But, let's say you learn to card count, which gives you a demonstrated edge. With that edge, along with good psychology and money management, you can be a long term winner – that's why the casinos will eventually ban you from playing – as they do not like players who have an edge!

The same applies with trading. When you have an edge, then all those other pieces of trading become important. Simply put, it all starts with a good strategy, and that is why I focus on algo strategy improvement techniques in this book.

I've broken this book into 4 major sections:

General Tips And Helpful Advice:

Chapter 1 – Is Algo Trading Getting Harder? – What does algo trading look like these days, compared to the past? And what does the future hold?

Chapter 2 – Full Time Algo Trading – Can it be done? What is some helpful advice to help you in this area?

Chapter 3 – 15 Algo Trading Tips – Tips I've learned over the years that will help you in your trading.

Improving Your Entries:

Chapter 4 – Bar Size Study – What bar size is the best? Which is the worst? And why?

Chapter 5 – Mean Reversion Study – I test out some popular (and not so popular) mean reversion approaches. How can they be used to create good strategies?

Improving Your Existing Strategies:

Chapter 6 – Risk Protection Techniques – How can you take an existing strategy, and make it more risk adverse?

Chapter 7 – Bull Bear Regime Trading – Does "macro environment" filtering of trades actually work? If so, how can you do it?

Improving Your Exits:

Chapter 8 – Which Exit Is Best? – Results of my extensive test on exits.

Chapter 9 – Reward/Risk Study – Is there an optimum Reward to Risk ratio? If so, what is it?

Chapter 10 – Exiting After Profitable (Or Unprofitable) Bars – Is this a good exit approach to use?

For each chapter, I give you what I call **"Algo Trading Cheat Codes."** I boiled down thousands of research hours into actionable ideas. This is really the essence of the book – taking what I've found, and putting it to use in your own testing and trading – without the need for you to do everything from scratch.

There are a few other topics that did not make it into this book, which you can find at my website:

Dollar vs ATR Stops – I have ATRs stop losses battle it out with Dollar based stop losses. Who will be the winner?
https://www.kjtradingsystems.com/algo-trading-tip-dollar-vs-atr-stop-losses.html

15 Price Patterns That Work – The title really says it all. You can use these as a starting point for your own testing.
https://www.kjtradingsystems.com/15-algo-trading-price-patterns.html

Should You Just Buy and Hold Instead Of Algo Trading? – A legitimate question, especially given the nearly always upward trend in the stock market since 2009. https://www.kjtradingsystems.com/algo-trade-or-buy-and-hold.html

Other research I share on my YouTube channel:
https://www.youtube.com/channel/UCjTZtWVBchDTJuxy_7GjySQ

By the time you finish this book, you likely will see other new research

I have completed and posted to my website. What can I say, I LOVE studying algo trading!

So, let's not waste any more time, let's get started!

"Algo Trading Cheat Codes" – This is the book you are holding now. It is designed for intermediate to advanced algo traders – traders who are looking for new concepts and research to help them create new strategies. Using the conclusions of the work I have done for this book, traders will be able to avoid some of the dead ends inherent in algo system development.

As you can see, my books run the gamut from introductory texts to advanced information. Hopefully you will decide to try out one or more of these as your experience level increases.

CHAPTER 1–IS ALGO TRADING GETTING HARDER?

When my first book, "Building Winning Algorithmic Trading Systems" was released in 2014, I thought my publisher was crazy for using the term "algorithmic" in the title. I felt "systematic," "mechanical," "rules based," or even "quant/quantitative" would have been a much better word to use instead of "algorithmic." Not many traders used the term back then.

Boy, was I wrong! Turns out the algo trading has exploded in popularity in the past few years. Just look at Google Trends results for "algo trading" search popularity:

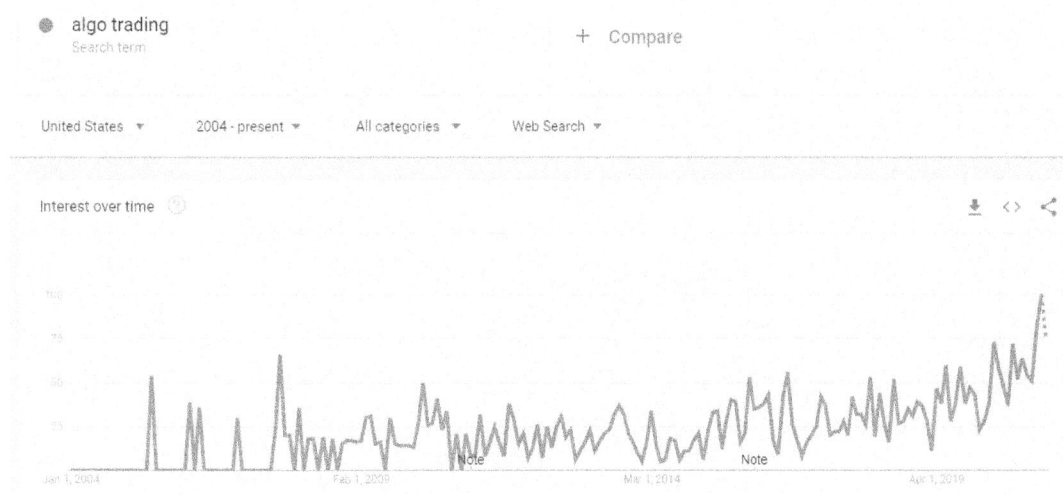

algo trading
Search term

+ Compare

United States ▾   2004 - present ▾   All categories ▾   Web Search ▾

Interest over time

Jan 1, 2004   Feb 1, 2009   Mar 1, 2014   Apr 1, 2019

In the past few years, algo trading has really jumped in popularity. It still pales in comparison to discretionary trading terms like "order flow" and "price action," but it is definitely becoming more well known.

Such increased popularity is a double edged sword. On one hand, more algo traders mean edges will likely be discovered and exploited by other traders sooner. The days of Turtle-like strategies that worked for many years are long gone. Just too many traders are finding the same profitable strategies via backtests. I believe the "shelf life" of algo strategies will decrease as a result.

New Algo Traders Are Not Always *Good* Algo Traders

On the other hand, from what I have seen, most new algo traders are doing things incorrectly. Let's look at a couple of examples.

Nowadays, there are at least 20 different trading platforms out there that support algo trading. 25 years ago there were only a handful. But most of these platforms encourage the same technique to find strategies: optimization. As even slightly experienced algo traders know, optimization is good only in small amounts. Too much optimization almost always leads to unrealistic backtests, and real time performance is never comparable to the backtest results.

Unfortunately, newer algo traders don't realize this, and consequently spend a few years in the algo wasteland of over-optimization. In futures, this is good for the experienced algo traders, since every dollar lost to over-optimizing participants is a dollar gained by a savvier competitor.

Another area where new algo traders are falling flat is in the automation craze. To simplify strategy development, many companies now offer "strategy builders" – automated software packages that produce randomly generated strategies with historically profitable backtests.

The problem is that many times these automated approaches produce junk. The strategies developed rarely work in real time. Of course, it usually takes the new trader a while to arrive at this conclusion, and again money lost by these traders benefit the better traders.

Yes, Algo Trading Is Getting Harder, But...

When you add it all together, it turns out that algo trading is getting more competitive, with more players entering the field every day. At the same time, while many will drop out, the ones that remain will be stronger and better equipped than algo traders of even 5 years ago.

As with any business, the smartest traders will evolve and improve. If you want to be one of them, here are some tips to stay ahead of the algo trading pack:

Start With A Solid Foundation

I've seen many algo traders enter the field and jump from platform to platform, try and fail with algo signal services and attempt every new algo fad, from machine learning to artificial intelligence to genetic optimization. The problem is they'll never get anywhere by continually jumping on the latest craze.

To be a successful algo trader, you really have to start with a solid foundation – a strategy development process that has been proven to work. With that solid methodology in place, then some of these other techniques may be incorporated into your process. But it all starts with a solid foundation – a proven strategy development process.

Try to Be Unique

Most new algo traders try the same things. 60 minute or other standard size bars. Signals based on the instrument you are trading. Stop and targets set at obvious chart levels.

One way to succeed is to distinguish yourself from the crowd. Instead of 60 minute bars, what about 59 minute bars or even 61 minute bars? As the trading day goes on, you'll get further and further away from what the 60 minute crowd does.

Maybe by having your signals occur a few minutes before everyone else, you'll gain some edge. Or maybe waiting a few minutes will flush out weak players (in a fast failed breakout for example). That is one way to be different than other algo traders.

Using other markets for signals could be a good way to go, too. Instead of using patterns in gold to signal gold trades, why not see if crude oil signals can be used to trade gold? When you start looking for relationships that are non-standard, you really stand out from the crowd. And maybe your performance will, too.

A third approach you could use is to try to get into the minds of less experienced traders, including newer algo traders. Look at a chart, and figure out where most traders might be putting their stops. Then create an algo to be buying when they are selling, and vice versa. You might find some edge in playing against the crowd.

There are many ways to be like the crowd in algo trading, and many ways to be unique. When you can, be unique.

Always Look To Improve Your Approach

I've been algo trading for many years now, and my basic approach to strategy development has not changed. That does not mean I don't keep looking to improve my process; I continuously do research to try to improve my approach and the strategies I create. Over the years, for example, I have steadily reduced the number of input variables I optimize with, and I have continually lowered the number of iterations I run in walkforward testing.

In other words, I put my previous contest winning successes in the past, and continually try to improve how I algo trade. In the dog-eat-dog world of trading, continuous improvement is an absolute must.

Embraced Planned Obsolescence

Nothing lasts forever, they say, except death and taxes. So, should you really expect a trading strategy to last for years or even decades?

While I have a few algo strategies that have performed well for over 5 years, that is more of the exception than the norm. The best algo traders may hope their strategies last forever, but they plan on them not.

For me, that means keeping careful watch of strategies, and turning them off (retiring them) when they start to underperform. Some recent research I have done suggests turning strategies off BEFORE they start failing. Sometimes it is better to just retire them after X months or years, regardless of performance.

For serious algo traders, this approach means ongoing development of new strategies. After all, there have to be new strategies to take over for the retirees! My approach to this is what I call the Strategy Factory®. This process keeps me developing new strategies, thereby staying ahead of the game.

The point here is you plan for the worst, but you can still hope for the best.

So, What's The Conclusion – Is Algo Trading Getting Tougher?

In a word, yes. But that is not necessarily a bad thing. Just like evolution, only the strong will survive. If you realize this and account for it in your trading, you should be able to stay one step ahead of the competition.

Algo Trading Cheat Codes

* Use a strategy development process that has been proven to work in real time, with real money

* Try to be unique in your strategies, bar sizes, etc.

* Don't rest of your laurels – continuously improve your trading

* Expect strategies to eventually stop working, and be prepared with new strategies ready to take their place

CHAPTER 2– FULL TIME ALGO TRADING

It happens every night. Right before you fall asleep, thoughts drift to an image of you lounging on a tropical beach, fruity adult beverage in one hand, fingers of the other hand tapping on your phone's trading app. Or maybe the image is of you sitting at your desk, in your pajamas, monitoring buying and selling of a hundred automated trading algorithms, all from the comforts of home.

That is the life of a full time futures/stock/crypto/forex algo trader, so you think. Or is it just a dream?

While many people imagine trading as a small piece in a glorious, carefree lifestyle, the reality is a lot different. Are you cut out for one of the hardest professions around? And if so, what are some different ways you can be a full time trader? This chapter answers both of those questions. To be clear, I am focusing primarily on algorithmic or algo trading here, but many of the points also apply to other types of popular trading, such as discretionary or chart trading.

Is Algo Trading Even For You?

To succeed in any endeavor you really need two things: desire and talent. True success is enjoying what you do for a living, whether you are a trader, a plumber, a firefighter or a business person. You have to REALLY want to be in the profession you are in. All that nonsense about loving the job you have is actually 100% true! Doing something you love will help you get better, to increase your knowledge, and to eventually become tops in your field.

Of course, having desire is not enough. You must have the talent, too. I wanted to be a pro football player when I was a child. The desire was certainly there. Unfortunately, the talent in my skinny, uncoordinated body was not there. Truly, you'll never get far without talent and aptitude.

So, how does this apply to trading, and algo trading in particular? Well, first off you have to have the desire to be a trader. Do you have a burning passion to trade? Can you handle working alone much of the time? Trading is ultimately a solitary "you against the market" existence, and that is difficult for many. Can you remain optimistic in the face of inevitable drawdowns? Most people cannot thrive under such conditions. That's something to keep in mind as you look to trade.

The second requirement is having the talent to trade, along with the required skills. If you are just out of school, chances are you never traded, so this is a big unknown. But for others, years of part time trading and strategy programming usually precedes full time trading. In fact, the dream of most part time traders is to become a full time trader. Having success on a part time basis certainly stokes the desire to trade full time – that is exactly what happened to me.

If you are in that camp, have you been successful at part time trading? Ideally, you want to have 2-5 years of consistently profitable trading on a part time basis to even consider being a full time trader. Do you not only love to program and test new algo trading strategies, but also do you have the skills to do so? If you don't have all that, how do you know you will even be a successful full time trader?

Possibilities for Full Time Algo Trading

At this point, let's assume you are confident in your desire to trade, and you are convinced that your part time success is a happy precursor to full time trading wealth and enjoyment. What is the best way to be a full time trader? Here are some of the most popular options.

Algo Trading, In Your Pajamas

When most people think of full time trading, they picture the beach or pajamas I described earlier. Certainly that can be true – as a full time trader I have awoken in the middle of the night and traded in pajamas before. But it is not as easy (or fun!) as it sounds.

To be a private full time algo trader, you first need a substantial amount of trading capital. The exact amount depends on the person, but let's assume you want to earn $150,000 pretax from trading. To do that, without taking unnecessary risks, it cannot easily be done (if at all) starting with a $5,000 account. Sure, some snake oil educators and trading room operators out there will tell you that it is easy. However, the reality is small accounts are more likely to get wiped out long before they have a chance to achieve huge returns.   (More   on   "risk   of   ruin"   right   here: https://www.kjtradingsystems.com/risk-of-ruin.html)

So, let's say you earn a very respectable 30% per year trading, with acceptable risk. That means you need a $500,000 account to generate the kind of income you desire. It also assumes that you do not add to your trading capital, which you of course might want to do (compounded returns are indeed a secret to wealth). All things considered, generating a full time income is no easy task.

As a full time pajama trader, though, you can always supplement your trading by ancillary activities, such as selling trading signals. https://Zulutrade.com is a site where clients subscribe to signals you provide, and if your trading is good, many people will flock to join. https://Striker.com and https://collective2.com are two other sites where you can sell signals to subscribers. All three of these focus on different markets (Zulu is primarily for forex, while Striker is futures based, for example).

Another route is to sell expertise via books, workshops, and other trading educational materials. While not technically trading, your trading knowledge and experience can help smooth your income fluctuations when the inevitable trading drawdowns occur.

Prop Trading

If you are starting out with limited trading capital, a proprietary trading firm might be a good route to choose. Typically, you will contribute a set amount of capital to trading, and the trading firm will give you additional buying power, especially after you demonstrate your prowess. But the competition is fierce, and many prop firms have shut down in recent years. The opportunities are just not as good in prop trading as they once were.

A   list   of   proprietary   trading   firms   can   be   found   here:

"We'll Fund You" Trading

In recent years, a new business model has entered the trading space. I call it the "we'll fund you" model, because that is what it basically is. Wannabe traders pay to audition for access to trading capital. For a few hundred dollars, prospects are given the opportunity to showcase their trading skills in a simulated environment. This audition is usually called a "combine" or "gauntlet."

The combine is a challenging test, with strict rules for risk management, profit levels and drawdown limits. Most entrants fail again and again, which generates nice revenue for the funding firm. Entrants who pass the test are usually given more tests, and eventually a select few are given access to capital, with a profit sharing split for any future trading profits.

While this model is enticing for those with little or no capital, it is difficult to succeed as a trader in this niche. Some firms in this space include https://TopStep.com and https://Earn2Trade.com.

Commodity Trading Advisor – CTA

Many good algo traders eventually want to run their own show and trade other people's capital. In the regulated futures world, this means becoming a Commodity Trading Advisor, or CTA. With this model, you'd trade client accounts full time, keeping a 1-2% management fee and 15-20% of the trading profits for yourself.

If you can show a successful real money track record, you should have no trouble attracting clients. If you had $1,000,000 in assets under management, with a 20% annual return, you could generate around $60,000 in revenue, which would have to support you, any staff, and outside services such as auditing and accounting. That is a pretty small amount of money, so most professionals agree that the CTA model does not become truly viable until you have $5-10 million under management.

When you start managing other people's money, the dynamics of trading certainly change. Drawdowns that might not matter to you matter a lot to your clients. Marty Schwartz, a great trader and CTA, described in his book "Pitbull" how clients were complaining to him while he was in the hospital, even though they knew he was deathly ill! It can be an unforgiving and ruthless business environment to operate in.

Plus, clients are not the only outside worry of a CTA. Government regulators are going to be knocking on your door, too. To be a CTA, you need to be registered and regularly audited. That gives assurance to clients that you will not disappear with or mishandle their money. You need to view the regulation and oversight for the good it brings to the industry. Information on becoming a CTA can be found here:

https://www.nfa.futures.org/registration-membership/who-has-to-register/cta.html

One big drawback to becoming a CTA, besides the headaches of complaining clients and burdensome regulators, is that instead of trading, you will find most of your time is spent on marketing and sales. The world will beat a path to the door of a good trader, but only if they know you are open for business. So, in trying to make trading – what you really love – a successful business, you ironically may find yourself trading very little.

Professional Funds

Of course, the "big time" for a full time algo trader would be a position at a top trading firm. You have to be smart, dedicated and usually experienced to get a job at one of these firms. Right now, PhDs in math, statistics and data science are in high demand, as trading moves out of the hands of individuals, and into the black boxes of computer code. Algo traders are really becoming the industry's dominant force.

Of all the full time algo trading possibilities, this is undoubtedly the toughest one, especially if you do not have a contact on the inside to help you. Your best bet may be to research a few firms, find out what their traders possess as far as experience and skills, and then emulate them. It is a tough road, though.

One trader I know took a unique approach that might help you break into a professional firm. He worked at a small Commodity Trading Advisor, and built a nice track record over the course of a few years. Eventually, he approached a big trading firm, using his documented track record to procure funding for his trading. It is sort of like the trading audition process described earlier, except on a large scale, and with real money.

Since you are reading this book, I assume you are an intermediate to advanced level trader. If so, you probably noticed a lot of the previous discussion centered on activities that were more than just you trading. Selling signals, offering trading education, running a money management business, etc. are all trading related, but more than just trading. Why do I mention these, if you just want to full time trade?

The reality is full time trading is pretty hard, not only to make money, but to make it consistently. I have had years trading where the first 10 months of the year were flat to down, but then November and December hit and were so profitable, it made my whole year look good! Doing other trading related activities is all about spreading your risk, and smoothing your personal wealth/income equity curve. If you have something trading related to offer the world (and not just offer to yourself), why not do it?

The failure statistics and anecdotes tell us algo trading is hard. Trading full time is even harder. It takes skills, desire and a passion for the markets. If you possess all that, there are different roads you can choose, depending on where you want this career to lead. But it can be done. The dream of every part time algo trader can indeed become a full time trading reality.

Algo Trading Cheat Codes
* Realize that the dream of full time trading is much different from the reality
* Make sure you are profitable on a part time basis before attempting to trade full time
* Consider outside trading related activities (signal providing, for example) to smooth out your personal net worth equity and income curves

CHAPTER 3– 15 ALGO TRADING TIPS

Before I get into the more in-depth research, I thought it would be helpful to share some great algo trading tips I have discovered over my years of trading and researching algo strategies. These tips will speed up your strategy development and will help the performance of your strategies.

Tip #1 – No Stops

To see what an entry alone could do, I usually test with a simple exit: exit after a certain number of bars, regardless of open profit or loss. This is a pretty good exit by itself. So, on quite a few strategies, I do NOT use a stop at all. Stop losses many (most?) times decrease performance, although they do give you peace of mind.

Of course, for any strategy you build, you might want to include stop losses, trailing stops and/or profit targets. Just remember though - this could DRAMATICALLY change the results you get.

Tip #2 – Work In Multiple Markets?

There are 40 or so major futures instruments in the US, and usually any strategy I create works well only in certain markets, or even only a single market. This is because NO PATTERN WORKS WELL EVERYWHERE. You've probably seen people touting "this indicator/pattern/strategy works in all markets, all time periods, blah blah blah." I think that is a load of BS, meant to snare people into thinking they have found the Holy Grail.

Why should a pattern that works in Coffee work for Gold? The markets are completely different and many of the participants in the market are different. There is no reason why the same strategy should work well in every market.

Some people say "the laws of supply and demand hold for all markets" as justification for all markets behaving the same. While the general law may be true, the specific ways supply and demand manifest will be different. Recent events have shown, for example, that the price of oil could go negative temporarily. Does that mean all markets could have negative prices? Probably not, since each market is unique.

That said, it is nice when a strategy works in multiple markets, but I do not consider it a "must." If this is a requirement in your strategy development, that is your choice. But realize you may be making development a lot tougher than it needs to be.

Tip #3 – Check Different Bar Sizes

Just like there is no "one size fits all" for patterns working on every market, the same holds true with different bar sizes. Some patterns work only on daily bars, some will work on multiple size bars. Just as with the market selected, you have to test different bar sizes and see.

While I'd be suspicious of a pattern that looked great on 90 minute bars, but fell apart on 89 minute and 91 minute bars, I would not be too concerned with good 90 minute performance, but poor 30 minute and 120 minute results.

Certainly, you might see this as really important, which is fine. Just remember it will be much tougher to find a good pattern that works on many different bar sizes.

Tip #4 – Always Include Trading Costs

One way trading charlatans try to fool people is by showing equity curves without slippage and commissions. What a joke! They will claim that everyone's slippage and commissions will be different, so it is appropriate to not show any at all. That is BS!

To properly evaluate a strategy – whether it is one you create or one you buy or lease – INSIST upon getting results with slippage and commissions included.

When you develop a strategy with no slippage or commissions, any optimization will lead to scenarios that trade more often (it is great to trade frequently if there are no trading costs involved!).

Of course, most people underestimate the amount of slippage they need to include. I've even heard people claim they get no slippage on market orders. Again, complete BS.

In my Strategy Factory Club, I require traders to use a reasonable amount of slippage, which varies for each market. These slippage numbers are based on both real world trading results and extensive number crunching (hundreds of thousands of data points).

The key here is to make sure you include slippage and commissions – ALWAYS!

Tip #5 – Lots More Testing to Do

Finding out if an entry is valid is certainly an important step. But it is one step of many in developing a trading strategy. I created 8 steps in my strategy development process. I have found that if I skip even just one step, my chances of having a successful strategy drop precipitously.

So, everything I show in this book is a beginning, not an ending. You really need to properly test and evaluate everything yourself before committing actual money to it.

Tip #6 – No Guarantees Of Success

I'm sure some of you will test the concepts I put forth in this book and end up with…NOTHING worth trading! Sometimes adding stops, targets or any other trailing exits you can think about will absolutely destroy the usefulness of the approach. Or maybe you use support and resistance to exit – you'll find that approach incompatible with many strategies.

The point is good patterns and indicators are nice, but they are just one part of an overall trading strategy. The interaction between entries and exits can be huge. Don't forget that.

Tip #7 – Don't Neglect Risk

I bet 8 out of 10 new traders just think about profit. I know I did when I was first starting out! But profit is only half the battle to good trading. Risk is super important, too. Usually, this is measured by drawdown. Think of a savings account in a bank. The account slowly but surely increases in value over time. No drawdowns, and really no risk (forgetting for a minute about currency risks, default risks, inflation risks, etc.)

If only trading strategies were like that – smooth and steady! Unfortunately, drawdowns are a major and unavoidable part of trading.

So, when evaluating and trading a strategy, remember to take a look at the risk involved. Focusing on that, and not the profit, is a great step in becoming a successful trader.

Tip #8 – More Optimizing Is NOT Better

A lot of traders think that optimization is "tuning," sort of like turning a dial to get better reception with a radio (this reference is probably lost on younger traders, but back in the day radios had a knob which you would turn to slowly change the radio frequency, and "tune in" a radio station broadcast). The more tuning you do, these traders mistakenly think, the better the strategy matches current market conditions, and the better the strategy will work going forward.

Tuning might work for a radio, but it does not necessarily work for trading strategies! Don't fall for this. More optimizing is almost always BAD. Try to optimize as little as possible.

'Nuf said.

Tip #9 – Remember, Patterns and General Findings Are Not Full Strategies

Whenever I reveal entries, exits or patterns I have found that work well, there are always a few people who decide to just take my work and immediately start trading it. That is crazy!

Remember, research presented here is the START of an algo trading strategy, not the finished product. My work will hopefully will get you on the right path, but there is a lot more work to do before you start trading live.

I always envision strategy building as a factory. Ideas and patterns are the raw material to feed the factory. The "machines" in the factory are simply the tests you run to develop, improve and verify the strategy. In this way, the factory churns out strategies, or junk for the scrap heap.

To keep the factory running, you need lots of raw material. That is what this book helps provide. But it is up to you to get it all working!

Tip #10 – Don't Forget Out Of Sample Testing

I have a strategy development process that works for me (and my students), but if you decide to create your own strategy development process, remember this: MAKE SURE YOU HAVE OUT OF SAMPLE RESULTS!

I use walkforward testing and real time evaluation to get out of sample results, and it works pretty well. Now, you might decide to do something different, and if it works in real time, with real money, more power to you.

The key is to do more than just optimized testing.

Tip #11 – Millions Of Iterations Are Not Good!

Many people have the mistaken notion that the more iterations you have, the better off the strategy. This is only partly true, at best.

More iterations:

1. Will produce a better performing backtest

BUT

2. Will also produce worse results in the future

So, if you want a great looking backtest use millions of iterations, as many as you can. But if you want a strategy that works well in real time (in the future), testing with fewer iterations is a MUCH better approach to take!

Tip #12 – Indicators And Patterns BOTH Work Well At Times

There are algo traders who think that only indicators – moving averages, RSI, ADX, Bollinger Bands, etc. – work with algo strategies. That is not true.

Patterns can work just as well for algo strategies, and many times they work even better than indicators.

The key, as you've heard me say many a time, is to test and see!

Tip #13 – Don't Forget Exits!

While most people focus on entries, don't neglect the other part of the trading equation – the exits. Exits can be just as important, if not more important, than the entries. Bad exits can decimate an otherwise good entry.

Plus, some exits work better with certain types of entries. You just have to try and see what works. Just remember that exits can have a significant impact. Don't neglect them.

Tip #14 – Psychology Is Important, Too

So much of algo trading is about numbers that it is easy to forget the human side of trading. Remember for every strategy you create, you have to be comfortable trading it. This means you have to be ready to expect the drawdowns to actually occur (most people ignore drawdowns until they hit them in the face).

In the end, it does not matter how profitable a strategy might be. If you can't emotionally or psychologically trade it, you'll never succeed with it.

Tip #15 – Nothing In Trading Is Guaranteed

Many traders have a skewed view of algo trading:

1. I create a profitable backtest.
2. I decide to trade it live.
3. I sit back and relax, as money pours in.

The truth is trading is hard, whether it is algo trading, discretionary trading or random guessing.

And all the testing in the world will not guarantee that an algo will be successful in the future. Testing helps, to be sure, as does a proven successful strategy development process.

But just remember, even strategies built correctly can and will fail in real time. Hopefully that never happens, but good traders are always ready for the possibility of things going wrong (which makes proper position sizing, money management, backup strategies and good psychology critical cogs in the trading success "machine").

Algo Trading Cheat Codes
* Each tip given above is a cheat code by itself!

CHAPTER 4 – BAR SIZE STUDY

I've felt for years that Daily Bars are the best for developing trading strategies. They are easiest to develop strategies for, at least in my personal experience.

That said, I REALLY like smaller size bars, both because you can trade them intraday, and because you can trade multiple times per day.

I'm sure I'm not alone in this thinking, as there are many traders and wannabe traders out there who feel the key to success is frequent trading. But is it really?

I decided to take a look, since perhaps I've been neglecting the fertile ground of small bars like 2 minute and 5 minute bars. Or maybe my focus on Daily and 1440 minute bars (which are not the same, due to settlement price versus last price traded issues – a whole other subject) has been right all along.

So let's find out!

Study Setup
I am going to look at a simple breakout strategy:

Tradestation Code
If close=highest(close,InputVar1) then buy next bar at market;
If close=lowest(close,InputVar1) then sellshort next bar at market;

I set InputVar1 to short (10 bars), medium (25 bars) or long term (40 bars). I selected a simple breakout approach because that is used by many traders.

I also decided to look at the opposite strategy. Think of it as a counter trend or mean reversion "anti-breakout" approach:

If close=highest(close,InputVar1) then sellshort next bar at market;
If close=lowest(close,InputVar1) then buy next bar at market;

For markets, I am going to look at 40 different futures markets (back adjusted continuous contracts):

@AD,@BO,@BP,@C,@CC,@CD,@CL,@CT,@DX,@EC,@ES.D,@E

I am running the test from Jan 1, 2006 to February 12, 2021.

Finally (and most importantly for this study), I am going to examine 25 different bar sizes, from 1 minute to 1440 minutes:

1,2,5,10,20,30,45,60,75,90,120,150,180,210,240,300,360,420,480,600,72

Since I am using only market orders to enter and exit, real life trading demands that I apply slippage and commissions to the results. As a theoretical comparison, however, I'll also run a slippage and commission-free study alongside.

My initial thought here is that without slippage and commissions, the smaller bar sizes will be preferable, but once trading costs are added in, the daily bars will be significantly better. We will soon see if I am right!

Results - Breakout Strategy, No Slippage Or Commissions
Let's first just look at Net Profit, and see which bar sizes are potentially the best.

Figure 1 - Profit vs. Bar Size, Trend Strategy, No Slippage Or Commissions

Below 10 minutes, even without slippage and commissions, results are poor. What does this tell us? Breakouts on small bars are usually false! That is definitely something good to know.

As the bar size increases, results get better, peaking at 120 minute bars. Breakouts of those bars are the most profitable.

The other interesting point here is that longer bars, from roughly 360-1440 minutes, are pretty much the same (and not all that great compared to the peak profit at 120 minute bars).

Taking a look at maximum drawdown, the smaller size bars have larger maximum drawdowns, up until around 60 minute bars.

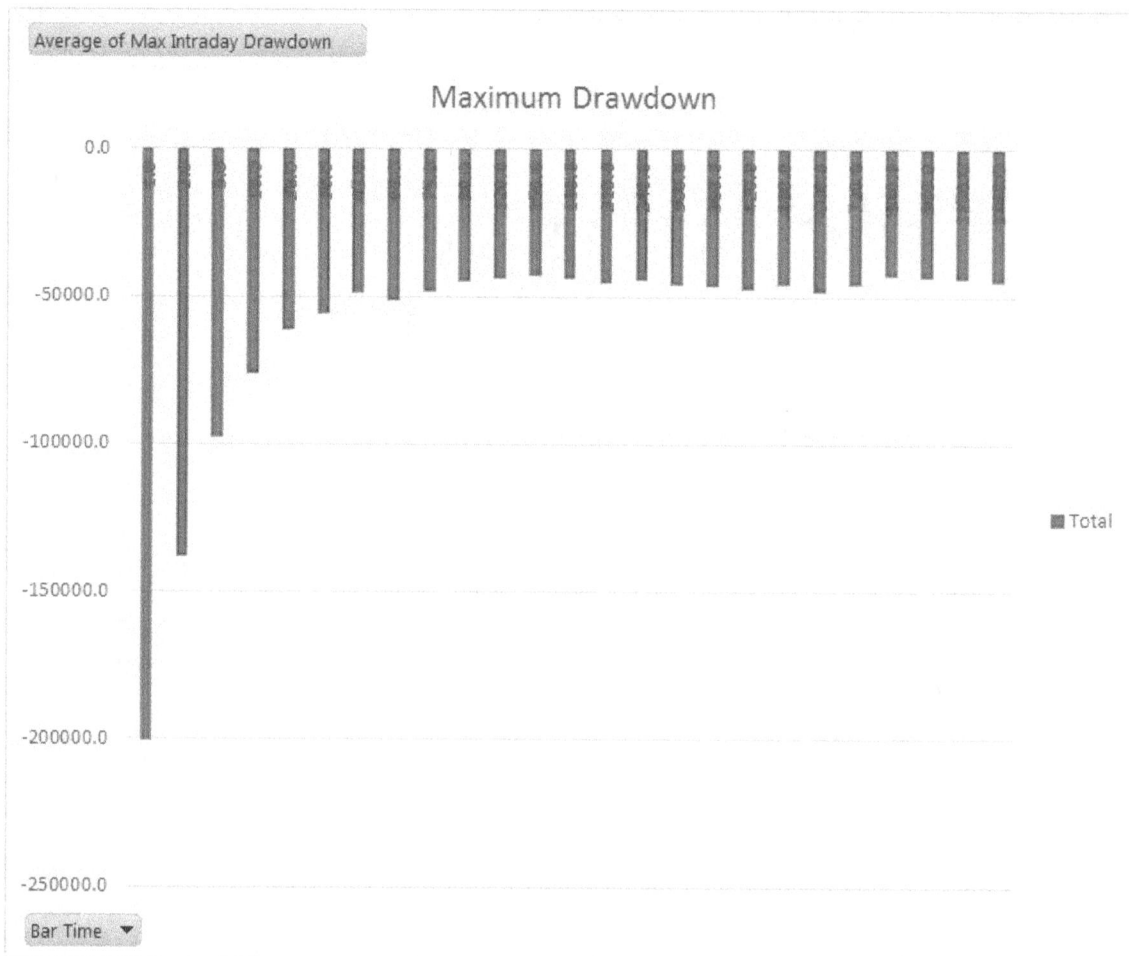

Figure 2 - Max Drawdown vs. Bar Size, Trend Strategy, No Slippage Or Commissions

So from this, it is pretty clear that very small bars are terrible for a traditional trend following approach, at least with the big picture of 40 markets. There are actually some markets (CT, HO, RB, S) where the smaller size bars are actually much more profitable. But in general, smaller size bars are worse.

Results – CounterTrend BreakOut Strategy, No Slippage Or Commissions

Without slippage and commissions, the results described above should be flipped for Net Profit. Are they?

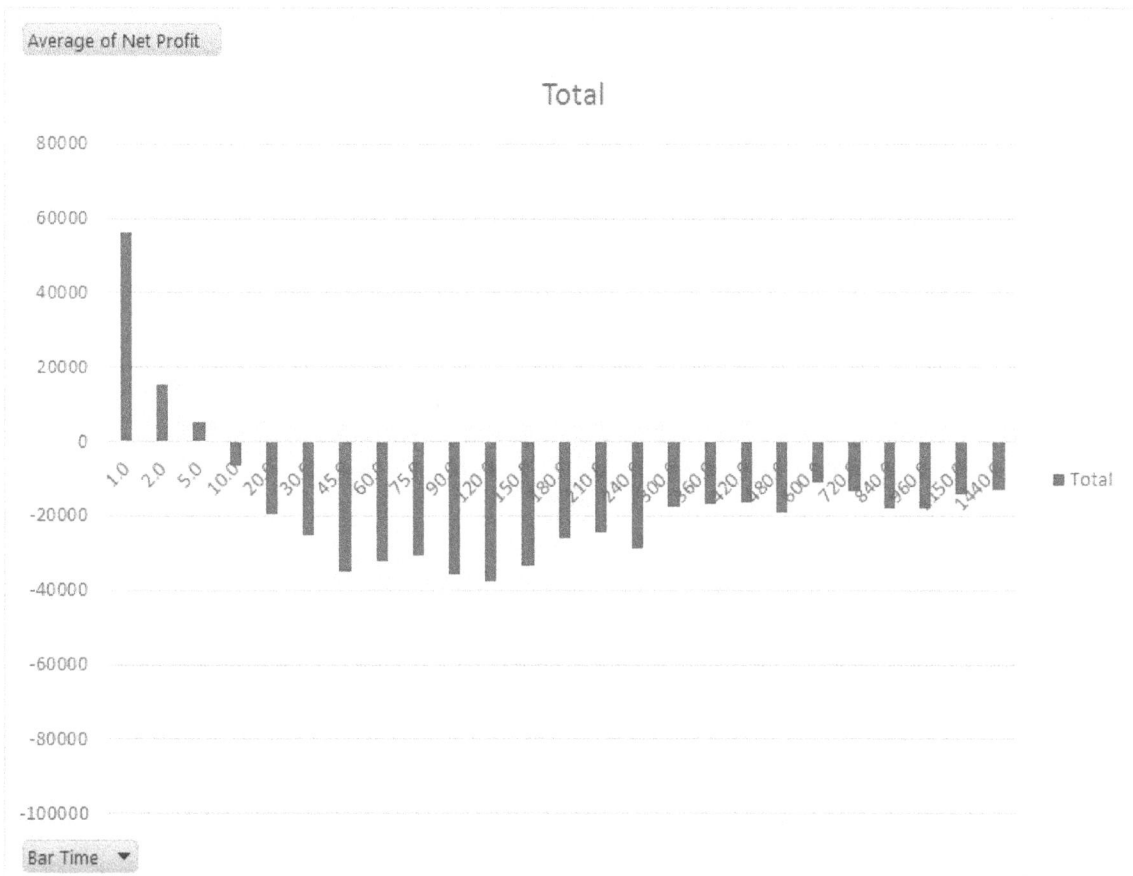

Figure 3 - Profit vs. Bar Size, Countertrend Strategy, No Slippage Or Commissions

Yes, exactly a mirror image, as expected.

For maximum drawdown, the maximum drawdowns still occur with the smaller size bars. This is a result of the really bad cases having high enough drawdown to overwhelm the profitable, lower drawdown cases.

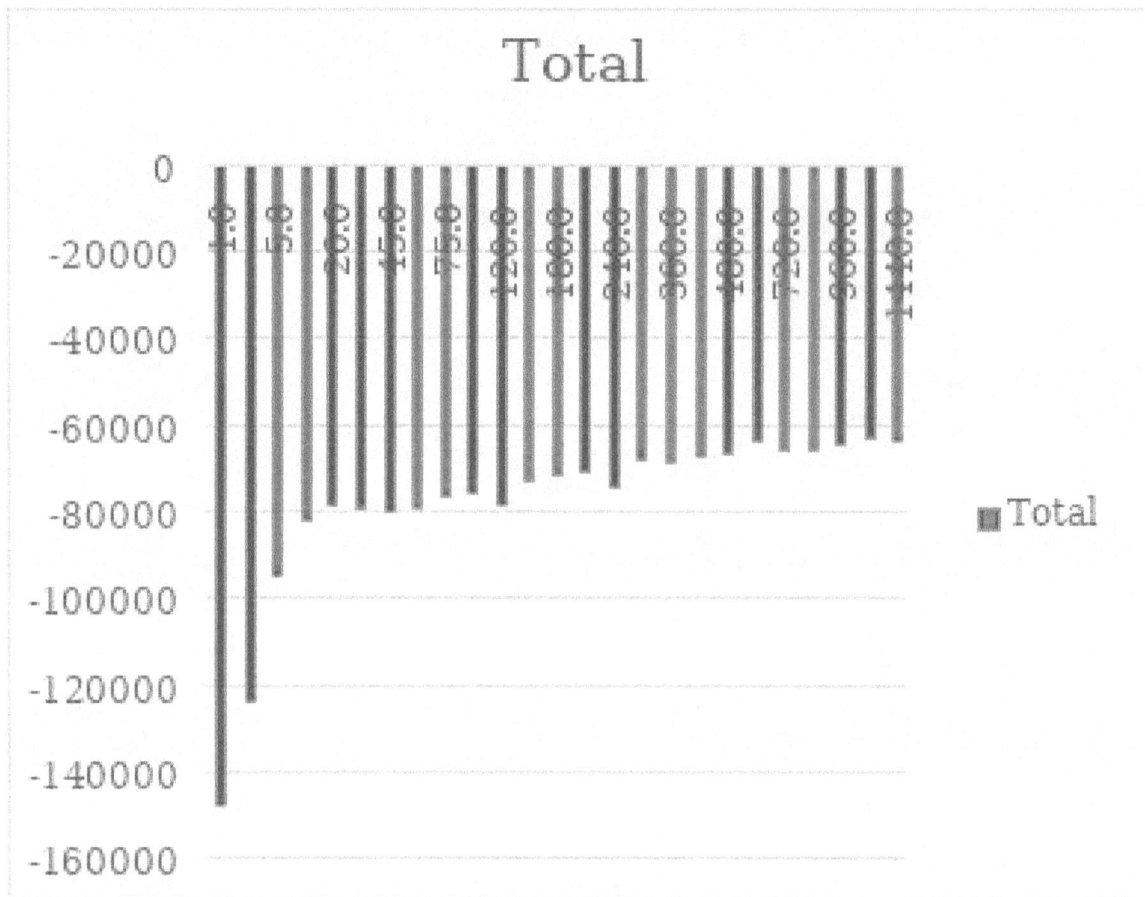

Figure 4 - Max Drawdown vs. Bar Size, Countertrend Strategy, No Slippage Or Commissions

Results - BreakOut Strategy, With Slippage And Commissions

While it is interesting to see how the bar size influenced results with no trading costs, the true test is obviously with slippage and commissions added in.

Let's first look at Net Profit:

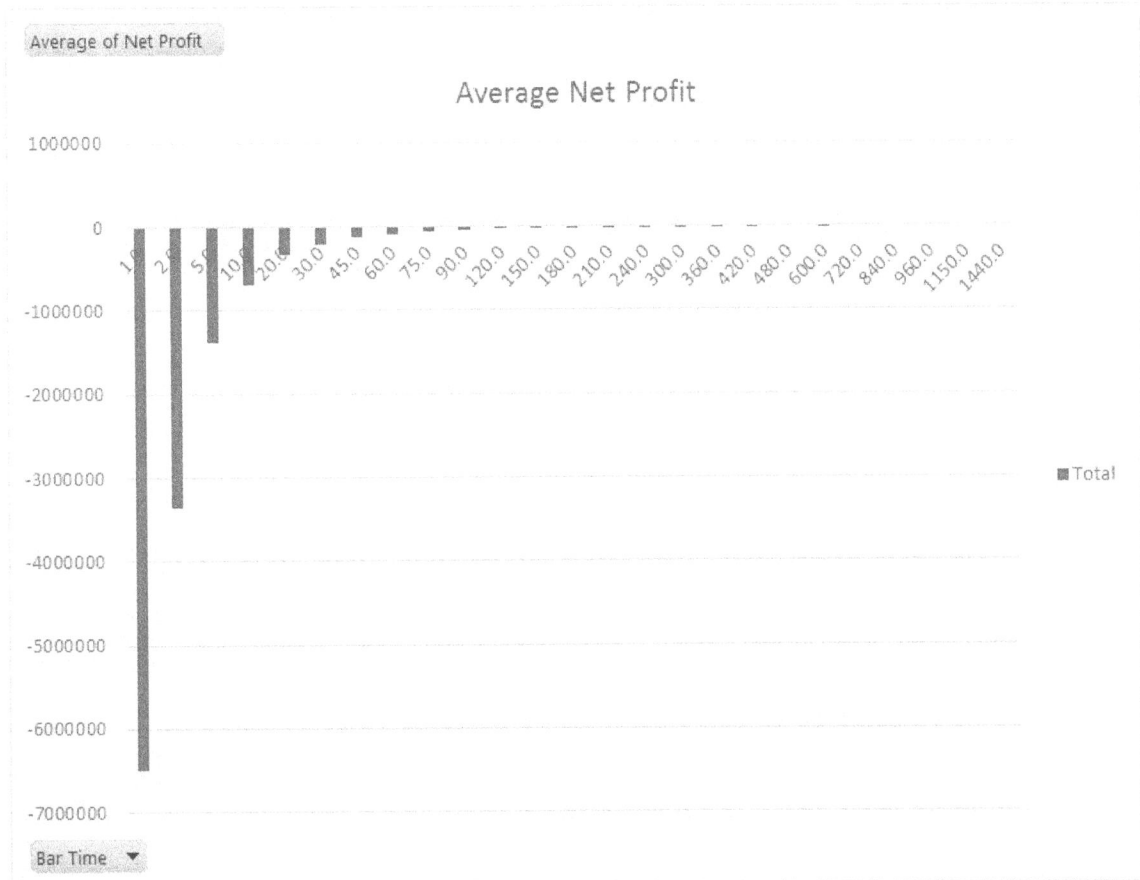

Figure 5 - Profit vs. Bar Size, Trend Strategy, With Slippage And Commissions

Enormous losses with small bar sizes! Those slippage and commission costs truly add up. Let's adjust the scale so we can see the rest of the bar sizes:

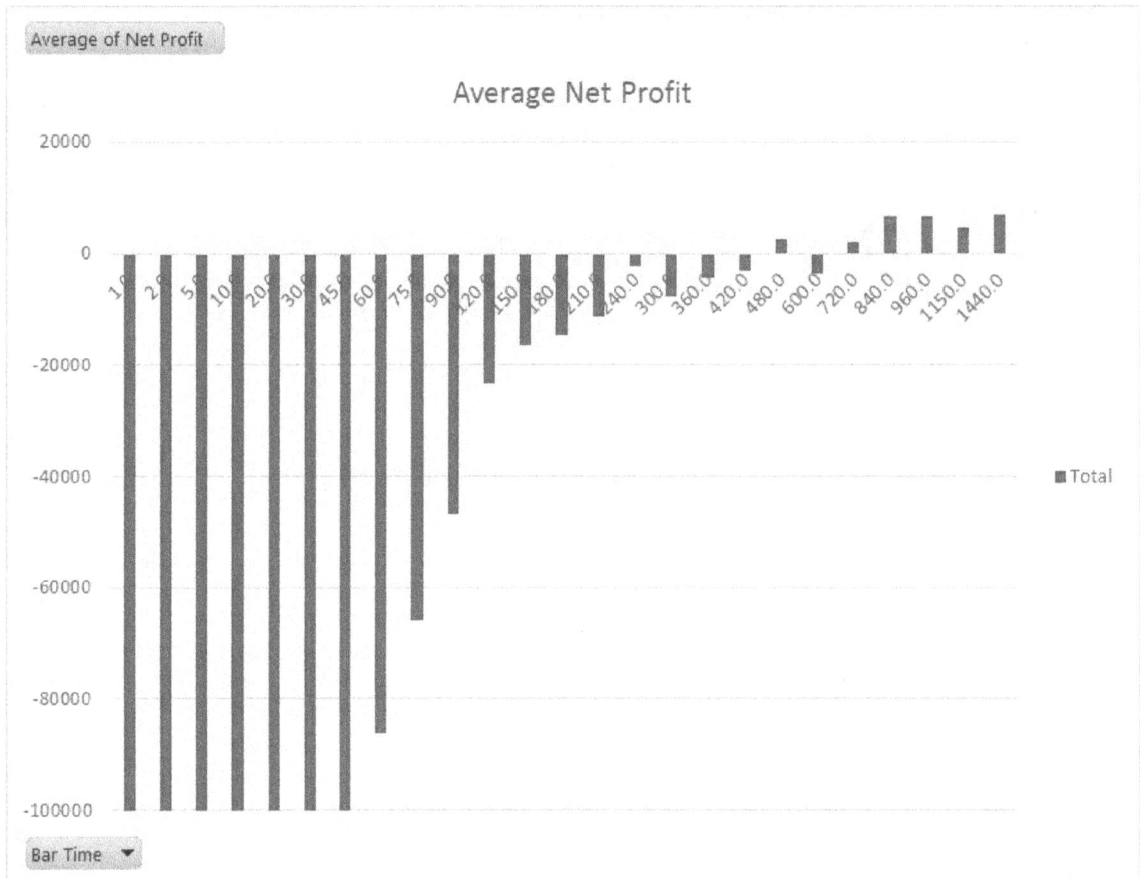

Figure 6 - Magnified Scale, Profit vs. Bar Size, Trend Strategy, With Slippage And Commissions

That is a lot clearer. It shows overall profitability with 12 hour (720) minute bars and higher, even after costs! The small bar sizes are really a disaster.

With maximum drawdown, we see much of the same thing.

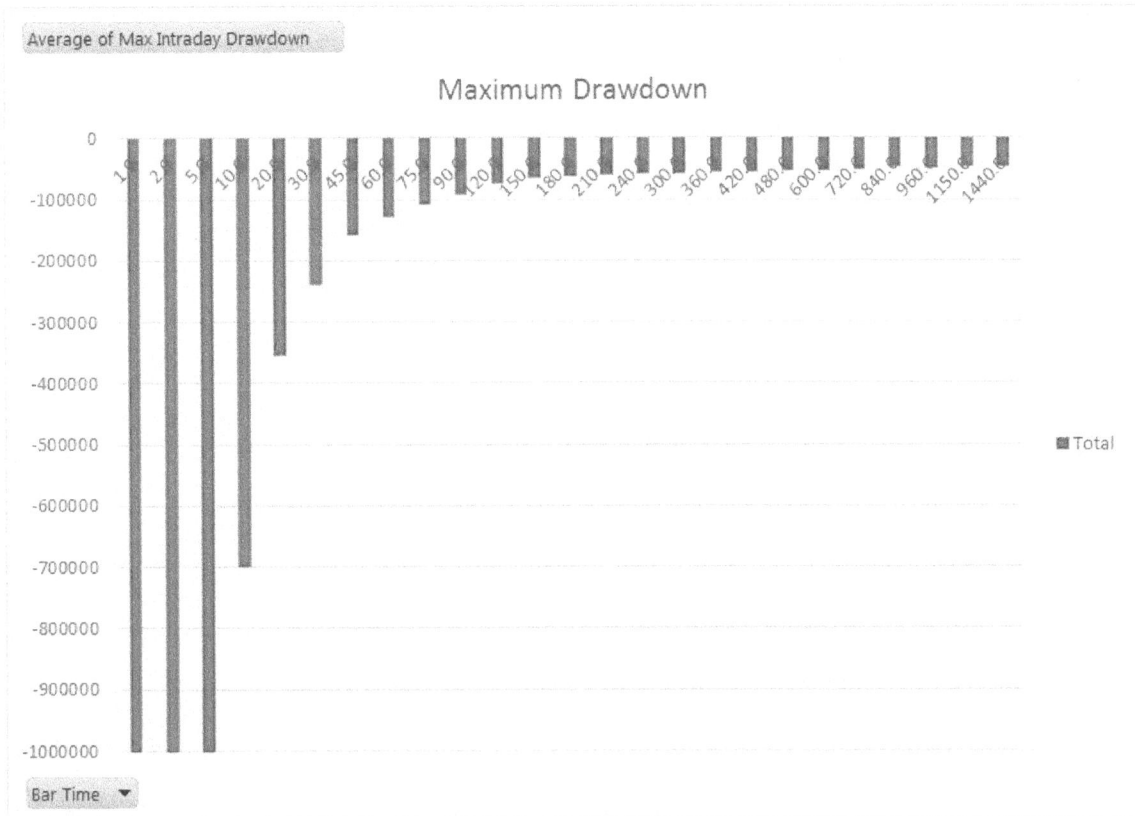

Figure 7 - Max Drawdown vs. Bar Size, Trend Strategy, With Slippage And Commissions

No surprise here! It is obvious that commissions and slippage are driving the results at the lower bar sizes, which is especially apparent in the charts below of slippage and commission costs.

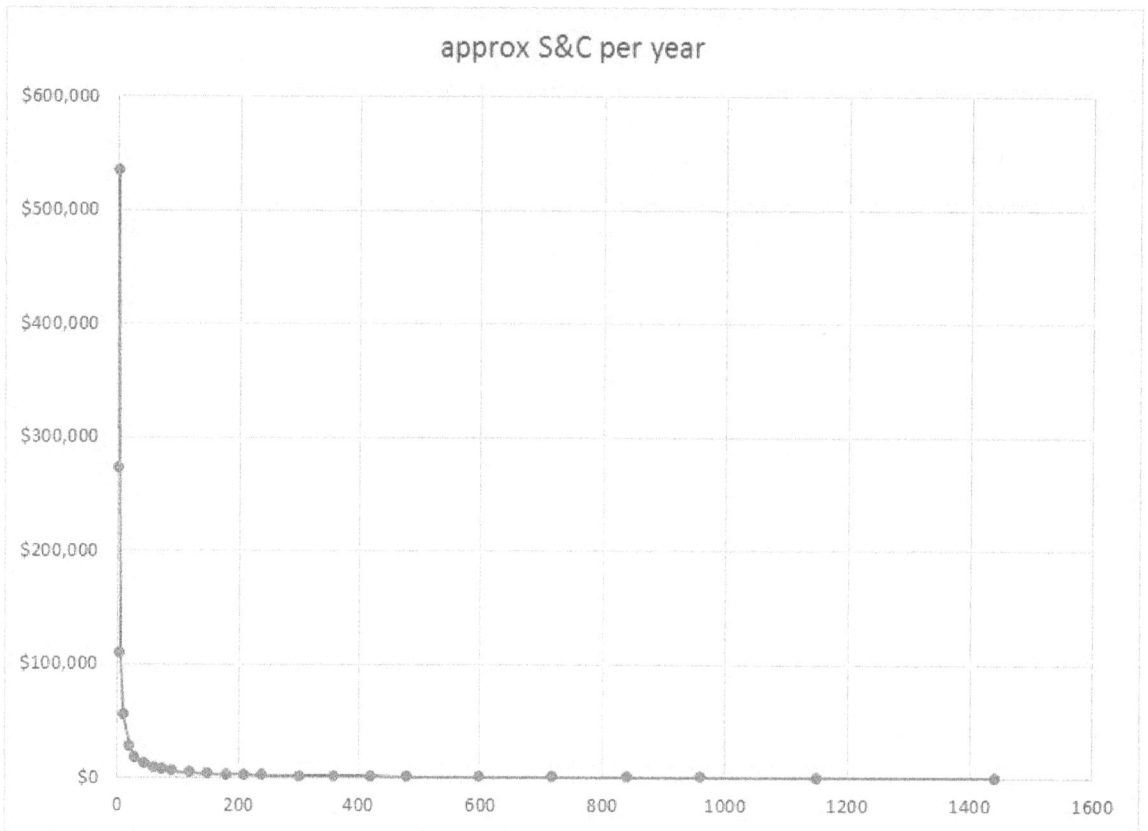

Figure 8 - Trend Strategy, Approximate Slippage and Commissions Per Year

With scale adjusted to show larger bar costs:

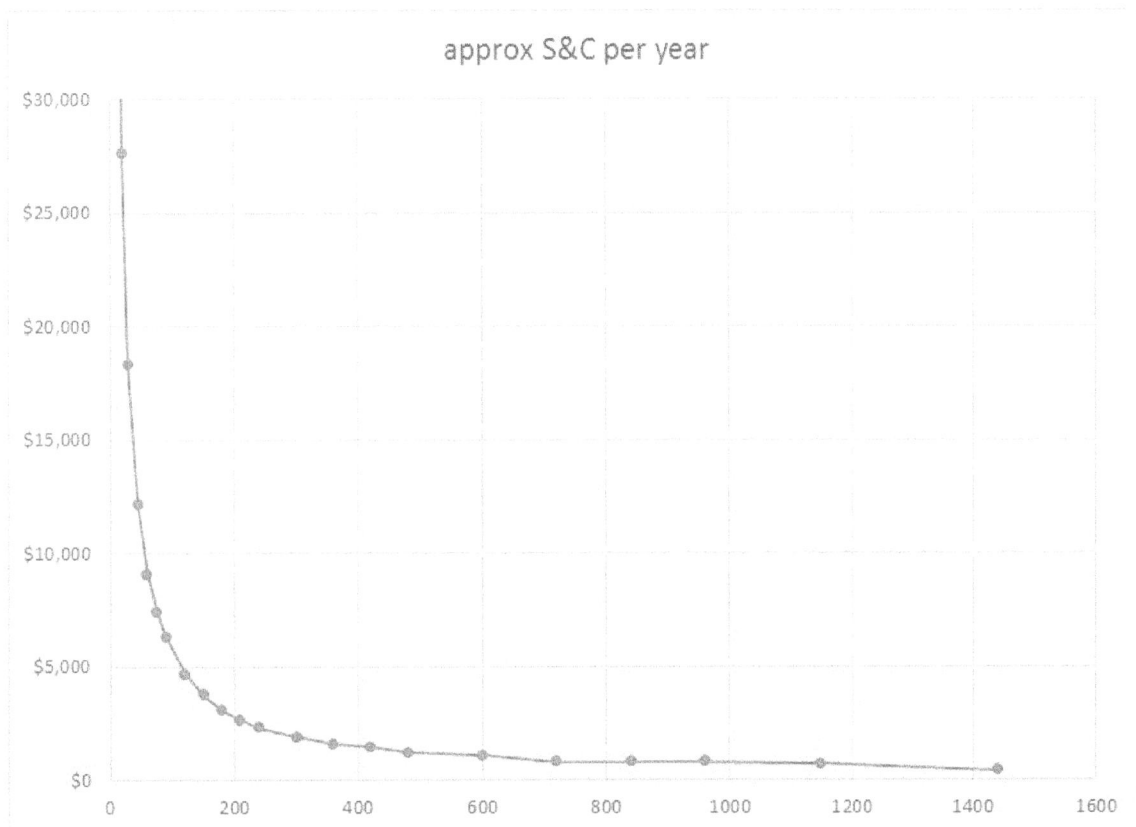

approx S&C per year

Figure 9 - Magnified Scale Trend Strategy, Approximate Slippage and Commissions Per Year

This might seem self-evident, but it is important to realize that more trades mean more slippage and commissions, which usually leads to less Net Profit. More trades is not always better!

Results – Reverse Breakout Strategy, With Slippage And Commissions

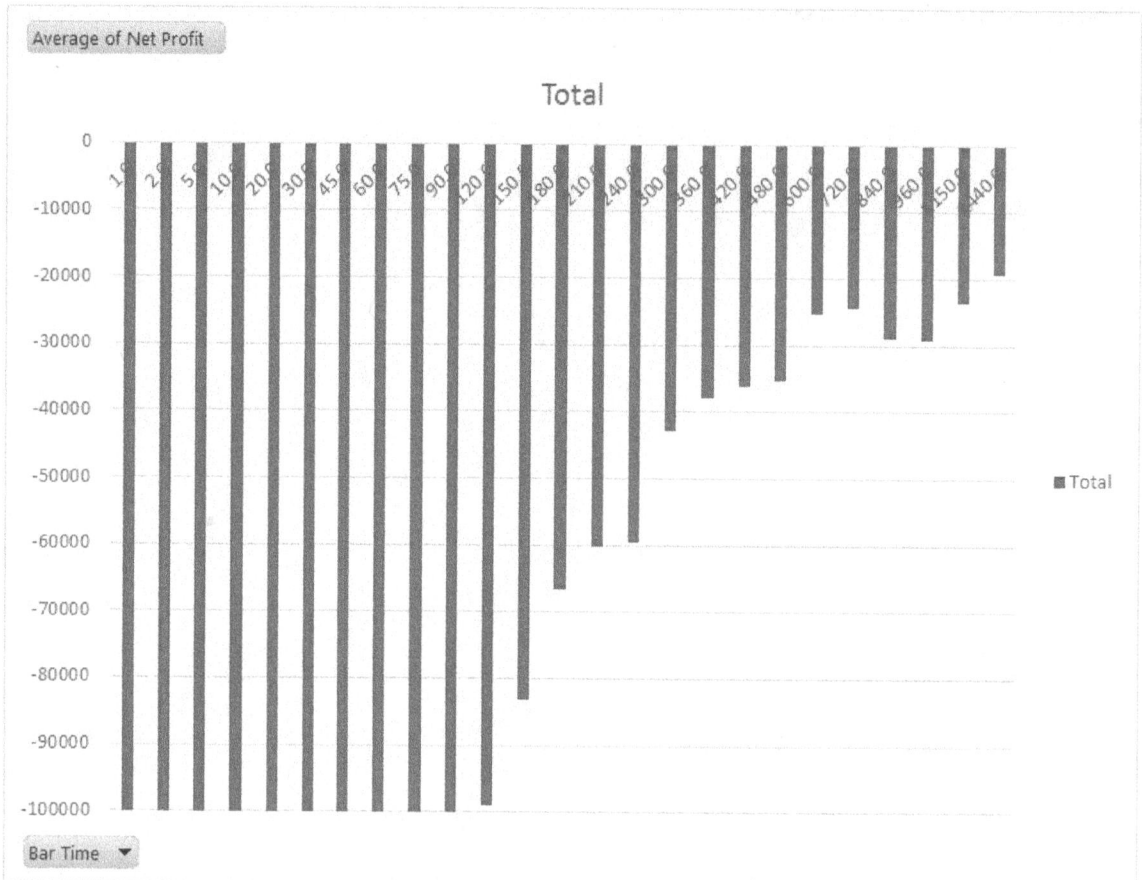

Figure 10 - Magnified Scale, Profit vs. Bar Size, Trend Strategy, With Slippage And Commissions

The reverse (counter trend) breakout strategy, on average, is not profitable regardless of bar size. This makes sense, since 1) the slippage and commission costs dominate the results and 2) in the few cases where the trend breakout strategy is profitable, doing the opposite will make it unprofitable.

Algo Trading Cheat Codes
* Slippage and Commissions can be a killer factor for smaller bar size strategies
* If you want to run smaller bar sizes, this study suggests more focus should be on reducing trading costs. There are really 2 ways to do this:

    1. Use limit orders where possible (just realize they have drawbacks in backtest and live trading, especially with "touch fills")

    2. Trade less! This study was "always in" – a better approach

with small bar sizes would be to have a strategy that was much more selective about taking trades

    * Breakout strategies with larger bar sizes can be profitable even after slippage and commissions. They may not be that appealing, though, on a risk adjusted basis

    * As always, use my research as a starting point for your own work. For example, if I was to look for a new strategy to develop, I would first focus on larger bar sizes

CHAPTER 5 – MEAN REVERSION STUDY

A lot of traders consider themselves trend traders, or mean reversion (counter trend) traders. Or maybe they see themselves at purely price action traders, candlestick aficionados or maybe even statistical arbitrage experts.

However they categorize themselves, everyone is ultimately a trend trader. If you buy at a certain price, you want the price to trend in a profitable direction until you sell. That holds regardless of how you might classify yourself. So, to make money every trader needs a trend in their favor when they are in the trade!

When you look at trading this way, all those categories I mentioned above just blend together into profitable trading tactics. Don't limit yourself to one style or category- learn how to do all of them well!

I bring this point up because for many years I eschewed what is commonly referred to as mean reversion trading. Many mean reversion strategies try to anticipate a turning point in the market. I always considered it akin to catching a falling knife. Why try to catch one, when you can just pick the knife up off the floor once it stops falling?

Of course, this is not good "trader think." If I can make good risk adjusted returns, maybe I should look into it, rather than just outright dismissing it. That is what I am doing here…

For this study, I am doing the same basic study you see in other chapters:
* 40 futures markets
* 5 different bar sizes
* 10 years of backtesting
* slippage and commissions included

For the actual strategies, I am starting with the work of Cesar Alvarez – he has a lot of good ideas at his website, https://alvarezquanttrading.com. I used his ideas as a baseline with sometimes minor changes, but other ideas I came up with on my own.

In all, I developed 10 simple mean reversion strategies, and they are described below.

Now, as with other studies in this book, I realize that a particular entry may not make money overall, especially since I am evaluating 40 markets and 5 timeframes. After all, my experience is that NOTHING works on all 40 markets and 5 different bar sizes – that would truly be the Holy Grail! My intent here isn't to say "use mean reversion strategy XX, because it works everywhere." Instead, I am trying to uncover mean reversion approaches which in general might be better than others. Knowing that, I can focus my full strategy development process efforts on the best mean reverting approaches. That is what I recommend for you, too.

Here are the approaches I used, with a short description and Tradestation code for each. If you do not use Tradestation, you should be able to use the "plain English" instructions I provide. Note: "Buy" commands first exit short positions before going long. "Sell Short" commands first exit long positions before then going short.

To make the testing a little easier, I standardized the optimized inputs as follows:

InputVar2= 5-20, step 5 (4 values)
InputVar3= 25-40, step 5 (4 values)
inputVar4= 0 to 1, step 1 (2 values) [off or on]
inputVar5= 0 to 1, step 1 (2 values) [off or on]
64 total tests

For all the entries, I have the following "exit 7 bars after entry" code:

if InputVar5=1 then begin
If marketposition=1 and barssinceentry>7 then sell next bar at market;
If marketposition=-1 and barssinceentry>7 then buytocover next bar at

```
market;
    End;
```

Note this code is not included in the strategies detailed below, but it should be added to the bottom of each strategy.

I chose an exit after 7 bars thinking that mean reversion trades should be relatively short in duration (approximately 1.5 weeks for daily bars). We'll see later how that assumption turned out (spoiler alert: not good!).

Strategy #1 – Simple Short Term RSI

General Idea:

When the 2 bar RSI goes below a certain value (oversold area), it is a good time to buy. Vice versa for shorts.

Entry:

If the 2 bar RSI crosses below InputVar2 then buy the next bar.

If the 2 bar RSI crosses above 100-InputVar2 then sellshort the next bar.

Exit:

If 2 bar RSI closes above InputVar3 then exit long.

If 2 bar RSI closes below 100-InputVar3 then exit short.

Tradestation Code:

```
If RSI(close,2) crosses below InputVar2 then begin
buy next bar at market;
end;


If  RSI(close,2) crosses above 100-InputVar2 then begin
sellshort next bar at market;
end;


   If Inputvar4=1 then begin
   If marketposition=1 and RSI(close,2) crosses above InputVar3 then
sell next bar at market;
   If marketposition=-1 and RSI(close,2) crosses below 100-InputVar3
then buytocover next bar at market;
   end;
```

Strategy #2 – Simple Connors RSI

General Idea:

When the 2 bar Connors RSI crosses below a certain value (oversold area), it is a good time to buy. Vice versa for shorts.

Entry:

If the Connors RSI crosses below InputVar2 then buy the next bar.
If the Connors RSI crosses above 100-InputVar2 then sellshort the next bar.

Exit:

If 2 bar Connors RSI closes above InputVar3 then exit long.
If 2 bar Connors RSI closes below 100-InputVar3 then exit short.

Tradestation Code:

```
If ConnorsRSI(3,2,100) crosses below InputVar2 then begin
buy next bar at market;
end;

If ConnorsRSI(3,2,100) crosses above 100-InputVar2 then begin
sellshort next bar at market;
end;

If Inputvar4=1 then begin
     If marketposition=1 and ConnorsRSI(3,2,100) crosses above
InputVar3 then sell next bar at market;
     If marketposition=-1 and ConnorsRSI(3,2,100) crosses below 100-
InputVar3 then buytocover next bar at market;
end;
```

Strategy #3 – Bollinger Band "Stretch"

General Idea:

When the closing price gets near the lower Bollinger Band, it is a good time to buy. Vice versa for shorts.

Entry:

First calculate the Upper and Lower (Down) Bollinger Band. Then calculate where the current close relative to the Bollinger Band window (=0 if close if at lower band, =1 if at upper band).

If close moves below the 10% point of Bollinger Band range for 2 bars, go long.

If close moves above the 90% point of Bollinger Band range for 2 bars, go short.

Exit:

If close moves above 0.4 of BB range then exit long.

If close moves below 0.6 of BB range then exit short.

Tradestation Code:

InputVar33=.0666667*InputVar3-.666667;

UpBB=BollingerBand(close,InputVar2,InputVar33);
DnBB=BollingerBand(close,InputVar2,-InputVar33);

if UpBB-DnBB<>0 then PercentB=(close-DnBB)/(UpBB-DnBB);

If PercentB<.1 and PercentB[1]<.1 then begin
buy next bar at market;
end;

```
If PercentB>.9 and PercentB[1]>.9 then begin
sellshort next bar at market;
end;


If Inputvar4=1 then begin
 If marketposition=1 and PercentB>.4 then sell next bar at market;
   If marketposition=-1 and PercentB<.6 then buytocover next bar at
market;
end;
```

Strategy #4– Moving Average "Stretch"

General Idea:

When the close moves far below an InputVar2 length moving average, it is a good time to buy. Vice versa for shorts.

Entry:

If the difference between the close and an InputVar2 length moving average is greater than a specified amount (meaning the close is below the moving average by a large amount), go long.

If the difference between the close and an InputVar2 length moving average is less than a specified amount (meaning the close is above the moving average by a large amount), go short.

Exit:

If close moves above the InputVar2 length moving average then exit long.

If close moves below the InputVar2 length moving average then exit short.

Tradestation Code:

```
InputVar33=.5*(.004667*InputVar3-.08667);

     If  -close  +  average(close,InputVar2)  >  InputVar33*
average(close,InputVar2) then begin
        buy next bar at market;
      end;



     If      close   -average(close,InputVar2)   >   InputVar33*
average(close,InputVar2) then begin
        sellshort next bar at market;
      end;
```

```
If Inputvar4=1 then begin
    If marketposition=1 and close>average(close,InputVar2) then sell next
bar at market;
        If marketposition=-1 and close<average(close,InputVar2) then
buytocover next bar at market;
    end;
```

Strategy #5 – Percent Decrease

General Idea:

When the close has fallen by a certain percentage, it is a good time to buy. Vice versa for shorts.

Entry:

If the close divided by the close InputVar22 bars ago is less than InputVar33, buy next bar at market.

If the close divided by the close InputVar22 bars ago is greater than 1-InputVar33, sellshort next bar at market.

Exit:

If close divided close InputVar22 bars ago crosses above 1 then exit long.

If close divided close InputVar22 bars ago crosses below 1 then exit short.

Tradestation Code:

InputVar22=.466667*InputVar2+.666667;

InputVar33=.0066667*InputVar3+.68333;

> *If (close/(close[InputVar22]+.00001)) < InputVar33 then begin*
> *buy next bar at market;*

> *end;*

> *If (close/(close[InputVar22]+.00001)) > 1-InputVar33 then begin*
> *sellshort next bar at market;*

> *end;*

```
If Inputvar4=1 then begin
      If marketposition=1 and (close/(close[InputVar22]+.00001))>1 then
sell next bar at market;
      If marketposition=-1 and (close/(close[InputVar22]+.00001))<1 then
buytocover next bar at market;
      end;
```

Strategy #6 – Bars Up/ Bars Down

General Idea:

After a certain number of consecutive down bars, it is a good time to buy. Vice versa for shorts.

Entry:

If the price closes down for 3, 4, 5, or 6 bars in a row (depending on setting) go long at the next bar.

If the price closes up for 3, 4, 5, or 6 bars in a row (depending on setting) go short at the next bar.

Exit:

Once the consecutive down bar streak ends, then exit long.
Once the consecutive up bar streak ends, then exit short.

Tradestation Code:

CanGoLong2=False;
CanGoShort2=False;

If InputVar2=5 and close<close[1] and close[1]<close[2] then CanGoLong2=True;
If InputVar2=5 and close>close[1] and close[1]>close[2] then CanGoShort2=True;

If InputVar2=10 and close<close[1] and close[1]<close[2] and close[2] <close[3] then CanGoLong2=True;
If InputVar2=10 and close>close[1] and close[1]>close[2] and close[2]>close[3] then CanGoShort2=True;

If InputVar2=15 and close<close[1] and close[1]<close[2] and close[2] <close[3] and close[3]<close[4] then CanGoLong2=True;

If InputVar2=15 and close>close[1] and close[1]>close[2] and close[2]>close[3] and close[3]>close[4] then CanGoShort2=True;

If InputVar2=20 and close<close[1] and close[1]<close[2] and close[2] <close[3] and close[3]<close[4] and close[4]<close[5] then CanGoLong2=True;

If InputVar2=20 and close>close[1] and close[1]>close[2] and close[2]>close[3] and close[3]>close[4] and close[4]>close[5] then CanGoShort2=True;

If CanGoLong2=True then begin
 buy next bar at market;
end;

If CanGoShort2=True then begin
sellshort next bar at market;
end;

If Inputvar4=1 then begin
If marketposition=1 and CanGoLong2=False then sell next bar at market;
If marketposition=-1 and CanGoShort2=False then buytocover next bar at market;
 end;

Strategy #7 – Reverse Breakout

General Idea:

When a downside breakout occurs, it is a good time to buy. Vice versa for shorts.

Entry:

If the close is the lowest close of the last InputVar2 bars, then go long next bar at market.

If the close is the highest close of the last InputVar2 bars, then go short next bar at market.

Exit:

If the close is the highest close of the last InputVar3 bars, then exit long next bar at market.

If the close is the lowest close of the last InputVar3 bars, then exit short next bar at market.

Tradestation Code:

```
If close=lowest(close,InputVar2) then begin
  buy next bar at market;

end;

If close=highest(close,InputVar2) then begin
sellshort next bar at market;

end;


If Inputvar4=1 then begin
  If marketposition=1 and close=highest(close,InputVar3) then sell next
bar at market;
      If marketposition=-1 and close=lowest(close,InputVar3) then
```

```
buytocover next bar at market;
    end;
```

Strategy #8 – Closing Range

General Idea:

When the close is in the lower part of the recent range, it is a good time to buy. Vice versa for shorts.

Entry:

Calculate where the close falls relative to the range of the last InputVar2 bars. The result is crange.

If crange is less than InputVar33 then buy next bar at market;

If crange is greater than 1- InputVar33 then short next bar at market;

Exit:

If crange is greater than InputVar33 then exit long next bar at market;

If crange is less than 1- InputVar33 then exit short next bar at market;

Tradestation Code:

Inputvar33=.01*InputVar3-.15;

if (highest(high,InputVar2)-lowest(low,InputVar2))<>0 then crange= (close-lowest(low,InputVar2))/(highest(high,InputVar2)- lowest(low,InputVar2));

If crange<InputVar33 then begin
buy next bar at market;

end;

If crange>1-InputVar33 then begin
sellshort next bar at market;

```
        end;


    If Inputvar4=1 then begin
        If marketposition=1 and  crange>InputVar33  then sell next bar at
market;
        If marketposition=-1 and  crange<1-InputVar33  then buytocover next
bar at market;
        end;
```

Strategy #9 – Linear Regression

General Idea:

When the close is below the linear regression value over the recent past bars, it is a good time to buy. Vice versa for shorts.

Entry:

If close is below the Linear Regression value over the past InputVar2 bars, go long.

If close is above the Linear Regression value over the past InputVar2 bars, go short.

Exit:

If close is above the Linear Regression value over the past InputVar3 bars, then exit long.

If close is below the Linear Regression value over the past InputVar3 bars, then exit short.

Tradestation Code:

```
If close <LinearRegValue(close,InputVar2,0)  then begin
 buy next bar at market;
end;

If close >LinearRegValue(close,InputVar2,0)  then begin
sellshort next bar at market;
end;



If Inputvar4=1 then begin
    If marketposition=1 and close >LinearRegValue(close,InputVar3,0)
then sell next bar at market;
    If marketposition=-1 and close <LinearRegValue(close,InputVar3,0)
then buytocover next bar at market.
```

Strategy #10 – Simple Momentum

General Idea:

When the recent momentum is down, it is a good time to buy. Vice versa for shorts.

Entry:

If close is less than the close InputVar2 bars ago, then go long next bar at market;

If close is greater than the close InputVar2 bars ago, then go short next bar at market;

Exit:

If close is greater than the close InputVar3 bars ago, then exit long.
If close is less than the close InputVar3 bars ago, then exit short.

Tradestation Code:

```
If close <close[InputVar2] then begin
  buy next bar at market;

end;


If close >close[InputVar2]  then begin
sellshort next bar at market;

end;



If Inputvar4=1 then begin
  If marketposition=1 and close >close[InputVar3]  then sell next bar at market;

    If marketposition=-1 and close <close[InputVar3]  then buytocover next bar at market;
```

end;

Mean Reversion Study Results

Before I reveal the results, it is important to realize that the overall Return on Account will likely be negative, meaning the strategy in total will likely lose money across all 40 markets and 5 bar sizes.

You might say "what use is this?" Well, first realize that it is nearly impossible for a strategy to work, on average, over 40 different markets, 5 timeframes and with a variety of parameter settings. It would be nice if a strategy was that good, but that rarely, if ever, happens.

Yet, if you subscribe to the theory that a strategy that works well over a variety of markets, etc. is a good strategy, then the results will still be useful. This study will show you which mean reversion strategy is superior to the others, relatively speaking.

Once the better strategies are identified, then you as the developer can start to look for the best markets or bar sizes to focus on.

As a first step, I filter out the infrequent trading situations (less than 30 trades in 10 years is what I'd define as infrequent). Next, I eliminate the high trade count scenarios, which are likely just quick or immediate entries and exits. Rather than rack up the huge trading costs incipient in trading many times a day, I just eliminate those scenarios.

Here are the overall results, listed by strategy number:
1 – Simple Short Term RSI
2 – Short Term Connors RSI
3 – Bollinger Band Stretch
4 – Moving Average Stretch
5 – Percent Increase/Decrease
6 – N Consecutive Bars Up/Down
7 – Reverse Breakout
8 – Closing Range
9 – Linear Regression
10 – Reverse Momentum

Row Labels ↴	Average of Return on Account
4	-1.2
3	-37.5
7	-42.8
6	-45.4
2	-45.8
8	-53.5
1	-54.0
10	-61.7
5	-62.6
9	-72.3
Grand Total	**-48.0**

Figure 11- Mean Reversion Study Results

As expected, on average all strategies are net losers. But, strategy #4 (Moving Average Stretch) is far and away the best, and strategies #5 (Percent Increase/Decrease) and #9 (Linear Regression) were the worst.

Another way to look at the overall results is to look at the number of profitable cases, those with a net profit above $10,000 over the 10 year period. The best strategies will have the highest number of profitable cases.

Looking at the data this way shows that strategies 3 (Bollinger Band), 7 (Reverse Breakout) and 4 (Moving Average Stretch) are the best, while strategy 9 (Linear Regression) is the worst.

Row Labels	Sum of Prof>$10K
3	1489
7	1288
4	1227
6	1060
2	916
8	879
1	872
10	583
5	551
9	284
Grand Total	**9149**

Figure 12 - Mean Reversion, Profitable Cases

A third way to look at the results is to look at Average Net Profit. Once again the moving average stretch strategy #4 turns out to be the best by a longshot. And once again the linear regression strategy #9 is the worst.

Row Labels ↓	Average of Net Profit
4	-13492.8
6	-43368.6
2	-43975.8
3	-52862.1
7	-64277.5
1	-65017.6
8	-70292.0
5	-89496.3
10	-92490.2
9	-106303.6
Grand Total	**-63239.96655**

Figure 13- Mean Reversion, Average Net Profit

Looking at all three tables above, the following strategies are relatively the "best:"

2 – Short Term Connors RSI
3 – Bollinger Band Stretch
4 – Moving Average Stretch
6 – N Consecutive Bars Up/Down
7 – Reverse Breakout

Later on, we will take all these and combine them in various "and/or" configurations to create new strategies.

So, if we stopped right here, I would conclude that the moving average stretch approach is probably the one most worthy of further examination. I'd also stay away from the linear regression approach.

Digging a bit deeper, maybe the results were influenced by the "switches" we tried. The first switch was an exit after 7 bars. It was either off (=0) or on (=1). Why 7 bars? I chose that because it was a small value, as typically mean reversion strategies are shorter term/duration trades; they are not long term trades. It is possible that you would get different results with 3 bars or 30 bars. I'll leave that to you the reader to test.

Sticking with 7 bars from entry to exit, the conclusion is not having this exit (BSE Exit=0) is better than having the exit.

BSE Exit	
Row Labels ▾	Average of Return on Account
0	-42.5
1	-53.5
Grand Total	-48.04220123
Row Labels ▾	Sum of Prof>$10K
0	5542.0
1	3607.0
Grand Total	9149

Figure 14- Impact of Exiting After 7 Bars

The second switch was unique to each strategy, but basically was a quick exit of long and short positions. Was that a good thing to have in the strategy?

Quick Exit	
Row Labels ▾	Average of Return on Account
0	-39.0
1	-57.7
Grand Total	-48.04220123
Row Labels ▾	Sum of Prof>$10K
0	6511
1	2638
Grand Total	9149

Figure 15 - Impact of Quick Exits

The results are pretty clear; the quick exit (value=1) is not a good idea.

When looking at aggregate results, I always worry that maybe some strategies really shine in a particular market, and those results get buried with the average performance.

For this study, in general, what works in one sector tends to do also do well in other sectors. For example, you can see strategy #4 is the best in most sectors, and actually is profitable in ags, energies and stocks. It seems to be consistently good across market sectors.

Average of Return on Account	Column Labels ▾							
Row Labels ↴	Ags	Curr	Energ	Metals	Rates	Softs	Stock	Grand Total
4	8.2	-16.9	22.0	-5.2	-45.4	-10.7	3.8	-1.2
3	-46.2	-14.4	-61.3	-56.3	-29.9	-57.8	-5.6	-37.5
7	-49.9	-21.5	-59.4	-58.0	-42.3	-65.2	-12.4	-42.8
8	-53.4	-43.9	-69.6	-73.6	-31.7	-69.2	-37.1	-53.5
6	-56.9	-19.5	-42.1	-55.9	-40.4	-63.3	-34.0	-45.4
2	-58.4	-35.1	-43.0	-63.1	-26.2	-69.9	-14.4	-45.8
5	-64.6	-45.5	-21.0	-44.4	-92.5	-64.3	-94.5	-62.6
1	-67.4	-29.5	-53.1	-64.5	-34.5	-77.4	-36.4	-54.0
10	-69.3	-43.0	-65.1	-68.5	-75.0	-78.5	-36.8	-61.7
9	-81.0	-78.9	-65.9	-83.6	-62.9	-85.3	-36.3	-72.3
Grand Total	-54	-33	-49	-59	-44	-67	-28	-48

Figure 16 - Mean Reversion Results By Sector

First Blush Conclusions

- Best mean reversion strategies are #2, 3, 4, 6, 7

- An automatic exit after 7 bars is not good

- Quick exits with mean reversion are not good

I would be remiss not to point out that the best entry may be partially and even primarily a result of the parameter values I used in the analysis. For instance, strategy #4 (moving average stretch) might be best because of the moving average lengths I chose, or the thresholds I used to define the stretch. I did try to use reasonable values for parameters for all cases, but different ranges for variables might lead to different conclusions.

Further Analysis

At this point, we could stop and have some decent mean reversion techniques to test. I am going to go a step further. One approach that Cesar Alvarez suggested was combining strategies. For example, you could add strategies 3 and 4 together.

This could work two different ways. First, you could make this an AND requirement. Meaning, strategy 3 and strategy 4 both have to be true to be a valid signal. This will produce fewer trades, presumably of higher quality, since there are 2 mean reversion techniques that must both give signals at the same time.

The other approach is to use the strategies in an OR configuration. Strategy 3 OR strategy 4 could be true to produce a signal, and a trade would then be taken. This produces quite a few more trades than the AND condition.

And while we are at it, why limit ourselves to 2 strategies combined?

Why can't we try 3, 4 or 5 strategies combined in various AND and OR configurations?

Let's first look at the AND combinations. To keep things simple, I only show results for the top 5 combinations:

Combination	Average of Return on Account
Strategy 2 AND Strategy 3 AND Strategy 4	35.9
Strategy 2 AND Strategy 3 AND Strategy 4 AND Strategy 7	34.3
Strategy 2 AND Strategy 4 AND Strategy 7	30.8
Strategy 2 AND Strategy 4	30.1
Strategy 2 AND Strategy 3 AND Strategy 4 AND Strategy 6 AND Strategy 7	28.2
Best Single Strategy - Strategy 4	-1.2

Figure 17- Top Combinations, AND configuration

Compared to Strategy #4 by itself, the AND combining approach can be much more successful. But what about the OR configuration? Unfortunately, the "OR" conditions don't seem to be all that helpful:

Combination	Average of Return on Account
Strategy 3 OR Strategy 4	-16.0
Strategy 2 OR Strategy 4	-20.9
Strategy 4 OR Strategy 6	-24.5
Strategy 2 OR Strategy 3	-31.6
Strategy 2 OR Strategy 3 OR Strategy 4	-32.6
Best Single Strategy - Strategy 4	**-1.2**

Figure 18- Top Combinations, OR Configuration

The results here are very clear – combining mean reverting techniques in an AND configuration is good, but the OR configuration is not good.

Algo Trading Cheat Codes
* Mean Reversion techniques are definitely worth testing
* Best approaches using a single Mean Reversion technique:
2 – Short Term Connors RSI
3 – Bollinger Band Stretch
4 – Moving Average Stretch (best overall)
6 – N Consecutive Bars Up/Down
7 – Reverse Breakout
* Mean Reversion techniques are more powerful when "stacked" together - just watch out for too few trades
Strategy 2 AND Strategy 3 AND Strategy 4
Strategy 2 AND Strategy 3 AND Strategy 4 AND Strategy 7
Strategy 2 AND Strategy 4 AND Strategy 7
Strategy 2 AND Strategy 4
Strategy 2 AND Strategy 3 AND Strategy 4 AND Strategy 6 AND Strategy 7
* Combining Mean Reversion techniques in an either/or setup does not improve overall performance

* Timed exits (at least for exits after 7 bars) makes Mean Reversion performance worse

* "Quick" exits using Mean Reversion decrease performance

* On an overall scale, rates, stocks and energies perform the best with Mean Reversion

* Ags/Softs by far are the worst for Mean Reversion

* As always: test everything yourself to verify

CHAPTER 6 – RISK PROTECTION TECHNIQUES

90% of algo traders out there build strategies the wrong way. How do I know that? It shows up in the statistics – most traders lose!

When most traders build a strategy, they have one goal in mind – maximizing profits. That's not necessarily terrible all by itself – after all, you need profits to make it worthwhile.

More enlightened traders realize that the risk (drawdown) is a key measurement of a good strategy, and incorporate that into their strategy building process. Most people would not like an algorithmic strategy that made $50K per year if it also had $100K drawdowns. Don't you agree?

You need a good ratio between profits and drawdowns. Thousands of traders around the globe use my Strategy Factory® process, and they find strategies with a good balance between profits and drawdowns.

There is another level to strategy building, one that many traders neglect – risk protection. The need for this became apparent to many people during the coronavirus scare of 2020. Very high volatility, quick and violent price swings, fast trends and quick pullbacks characterized many markets, not just equities.

Just look at a few markets from late February 2020:

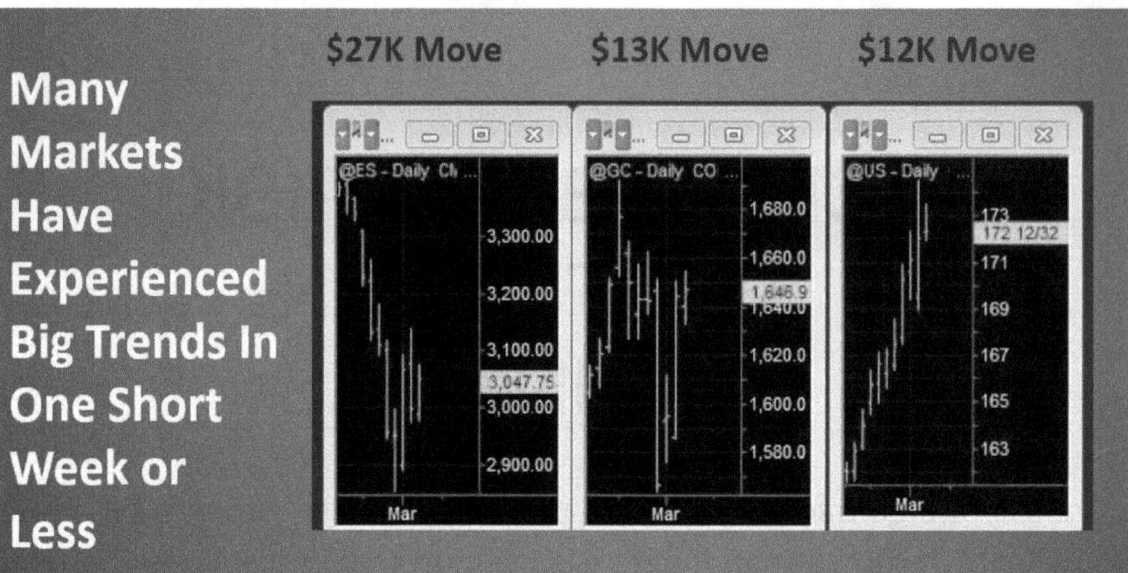

Figure 19- Big Moves During Times Of Turbulence

During crazy times like this, maybe just surviving becomes the primary goal, rather than making money. That is what this chapter is all about – techniques to reduce risk on an individual strategy level. I'll discuss and give examples of:

Daily Loss Limiters
Next Trade Delay
Taking Weekends Off
A High Volatility Kill Switch

I'll be discussing the concepts, showing you some examples, providing code and generally giving you the tools and knowledge to incorporate these "risk managers" into your trading strategies. With that, let's get started.

Baseline Strategy

For this study, I created a simple pullback type strategy, and applied it to 120 minute Crude Oil bars over the last 5 years.

NOTE: This strategy is for study purposes only. I am not saying this is a good strategy to trade.

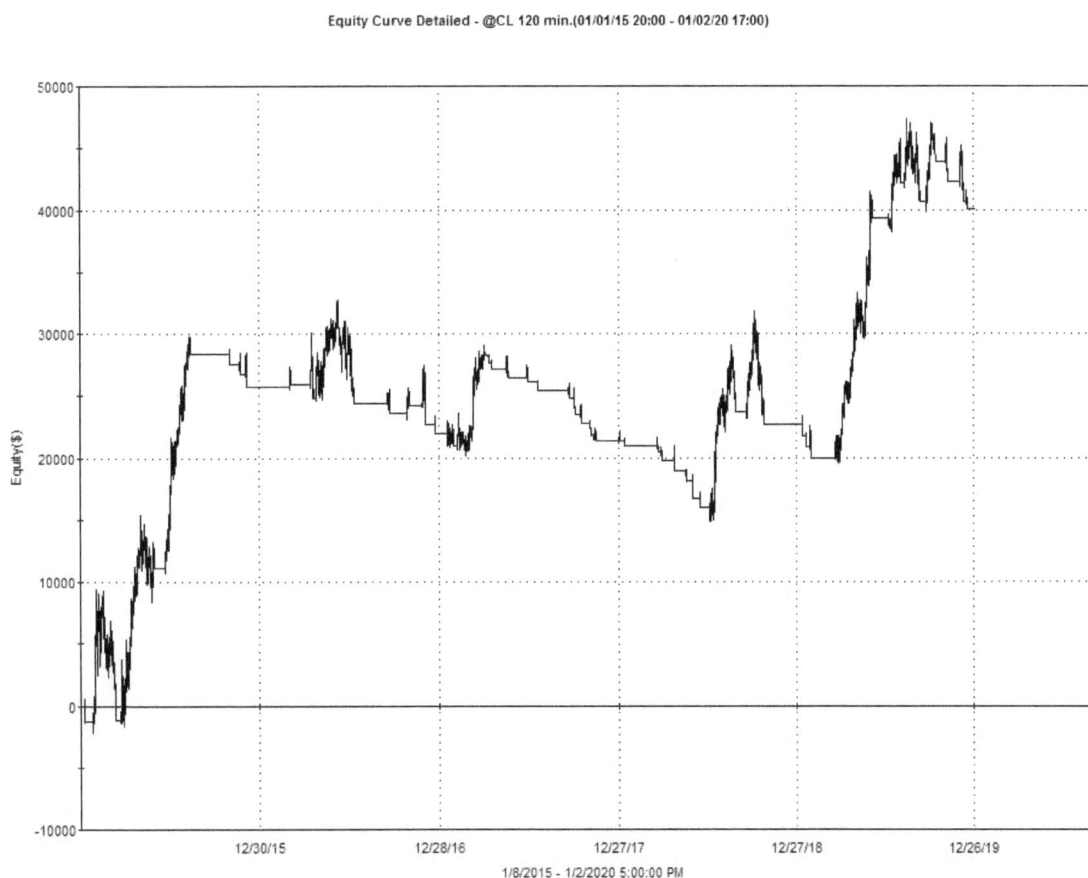

Figure 20 - Sample Strategy For This Study

Although this strategy makes a decent amount of money during the 5 year period, it has significant and prolonged drawdowns. These will be useful to see if any of the risk protection measures can improve the strategy.

The strategy itself requires a long term uptrend, and a shorter term downtrend, in order to enter a long position. Vice versa for short positions.

It also includes an ATR based stop, with a ceiling of $3000 per contract. This type of stop was examined in a bonus article on stop losses, which you can find on my website.

All the code below is in Tradestation format, but here are simple "plain English" instructions.

Plain English Rules

If the close crosses above the close "lookback" bars ago, and the close crosses below the close .5*"lookback" bars ago, go long. Vice versa for short trades.

The stop should be a multiple of Average True Range, with a maximum amount of $3000 per contract.

For this study, lookback was set to 10, and the ATR multiplier was set to 2. REMINDER: This strategy is for study purposes only. I am not saying this is a good strategy to trade.

Tradestation Code

```
//*********************************************
//
//www.kjtradingsystems.com
//Risk Protection Study
//Kevin Davey - STRATEGY #1 - Baseline Strategy
//kdavey@kjtradingsystems.com
//
//*********************************************
//

input: lookback(10),stopATR(2);

If close crosses above close[lookback] and close crosses below close[.5*lookback] then buy next bar at market;
If close crosses below close[lookback] and close crosses above close[.5*lookback]  then sellshort next bar at market;

var:NewStop(3000);
NewStop=StopATR*AvgTrueRange(14)*BigPointValue;
If NewStop>3000 then NewStop=3000;
```

If StopATR<>0 then SetStopLoss(NewStop);

Some important statistics for the baseline strategy:

Performance Metric	Baseline Result
Net Profit	$40,030
Number of Trades	92
Return On Account	280.7%
Percent Time In Market	34.1%
Max Drawdown (Closed Trade)	-$14,260

Figure 21- Baseline Strategy Statistics

Risk Protection #1 – Daily Loss Limiter

All traders like to avoid losing days, right? But experienced traders know that is not possible. So, the next best thing is to limit the loss on really bad days. This can be a psychological life saver, and possibly an account saver.

The version created for this study calculates the loss since midnight (chart time), exits all trades and prevents new trades if the loss exceeds a certain threshold. This works well for X minute based bars.

Plain English Rules

Every day, calculate the total open equity plus closed equity for the strategy at the last bar before midnight. If during the next day, the current total equity minus the "midnight" equity is less than "equitylosslimit" exit all current positions and do not take any new trades.

Tradestation Code

```
//*********************************************
//
//www.kjtradingsystems.com
//Risk Protection Study
//Kevin Davey – Risk Protection #1 – Daily Loss Limiter
//kdavey@kjtradingsystems.com
//
//*********************************************
//
input: lookback(10),stopATR(2),EquityLossLimit(1000);
var:EndDayEquity(0),CanTrade(True),CurrentEquity(0);

CurrentEquity=NetProfit+OpenPositionProfit;
If date<>date[1] then begin
EndDayEquity=CurrentEquity[1];
end;
CanTrade=True;
```

If NetProfit+OpenPositionProfit-EndDayEquity<-EquityLossLimit then CanTrade=False;

If CanTrade=True then begin
If close crosses above close[lookback] and close crosses below close[.5*lookback] then buy next bar at market;
If close crosses below close[lookback] and close crosses above close[.5*lookback] then sellshort next bar at market;

var:NewStop(3000);
NewStop=StopATR*AvgTrueRange(14)*BigPointValue;
If NewStop>3000 then NewStop=3000;

If StopATR<>0 then SetStopLoss(NewStop);
end;

If CanTrade=False then begin
Sell ("DLL-L Exit") next bar at market;
BuyToCover ("DLL-S Exit") next bar at market;
end;

If you use daily bars, you can use a stoploss statement instead:

Sell next bar at close – xxx stop; //xxx is the price where daily loss limit would be hit

Results

To see the impact this Daily Loss limit had, I varied the daily loss limit from \$500 to \$10,000. At small daily losses, the performance of the strategy is definitely worse that the baseline profit of \$40K. This makes sense, since with small loss limits, the market volatility will frequently lead to turning the system off.

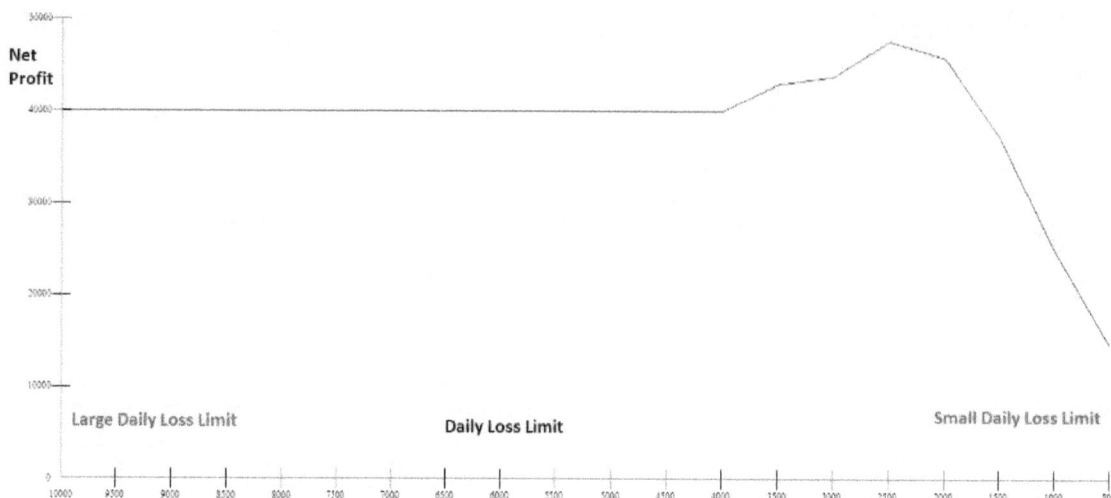

Figure 22 - Results Of Daily Loss Limit Study

From around $2000-$4000, the daily loss limit somewhat improves the performance, although not tremendously. Above $4000, the daily loss limit is never activated. So, the optimum result for the Daily Loss Limit is shown below:

Performance Metric	Baseline Result	Daily Loss Limit (optimum value = $2500)
Net Profit	$40,030	$47,675
Number of Trades	92	95
Return On Account	280.7%	344.7%
Percent Time In Market	34.1%	32.0%
Max Drawdown (Closed Trade)	-$14,260	-$13,830

Figure 23 - Daily Loss Limit Results (Green/Light Gray Is Better)

Looking at the results, you might conclude that the Daily Loss Limiter is good to have. But BEWARE! This is an optimized result. The $2500 limit is likely NOT to be the best daily limit going forward.

Recommendation

If you want to use a Daily Loss Limit, decide on the value to use BEFORE you run the backtest. Don't necessarily expect a performance improvement, but instead use it because you like the psychological comfort of limiting your daily loss. Any performance improvement should be considered a bonus.

Risk Protection #2 – Have Delay After Losing Trade

Have you ever had a strategy that seemed to get "stuck" in a rut of losing trade after losing trade? Perhaps it was a counter trend strategy, constantly trying to go short in a bull market. I've definitely had strategies like that.

One way to minimize the damage (again, psychological and financial) is to put a delay on any signal after a loss. For example, once a losing trade is closed, wait 5 bars before taking another trade. This should give you some protection from the "catching a falling knife" syndrome – trying to trade against a trend.

Plain English Rules

After a losing trade, wait NextTradeDelay bars before taking the next trade.

Tradestation Code

```
//*******************************************
//
//www.kjtradingsystems.com
//Risk Protection Study
//Kevin Davey - Risk Protection #2 - Delayed Signal After Loss
//kdavey@kjtradingsystems.com
//
//*******************************************
//
input: lookback(10),stopATR(2),NextTradeDelay(1);
var:CanTrade(True);


CanTrade=True;
If (positionprofit(1)<0 and barssinceexit(1)<NextTradeDelay) then
```

CanTrade=False;

If CanTrade=True then begin
If close crosses above close[lookback] and close crosses below close[.5*lookback] then buy next bar at market;
If close crosses below close[lookback] and close crosses above close[.5*lookback] then sellshort next bar at market;

var:NewStop(3000);
NewStop=StopATR*AvgTrueRange(14)*BigPointValue;
If NewStop>3000 then NewStop=3000;

If StopATR<>0 then SetStopLoss(NewStop);

end;

Results
For this particular strategy, putting a delay on the signal after a loss does not improve things at all. In fact, it almost always makes performance worse, especially if the delay is significant (10 or more bars).

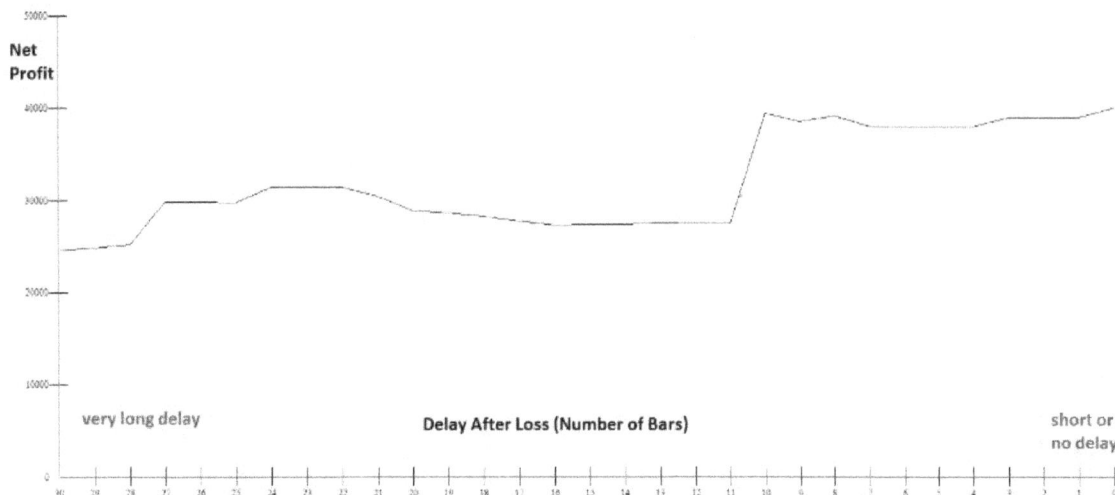

Figure 24 - Impact of Delaying Trades After a Loss

Performance Metric	Baseline Result	Exit Delay (optimum value = 10 bars)
Net Profit	$40,030	$39,445
Number of Trades	92	89
Return On Account	280.7%	256%
Percent Time In Market	34.1%	32.0%
Max Drawdown (Closed Trade)	-$14,260	$15,400

Figure 25 - Delay After Loss Results (Green/Light Gray Is Better)

Recommendation

This type of risk protection is really suited for strategies where there is a potential for many consecutive losses. A counter trend strategy would be a good example. As with any of these risk protection techniques, it is best to incorporate the rule in the strategy BEFORE you backtest. Adding the rule after you see initial results is basically cheating the backtest.

I would feel comfortable using this approach on a strategy that I knew was designed to trade counter to the major trend.

Risk Protection #3 – No Open Trades Over Weekends

Imagine one of your algo strategies trades Crude Oil. On Friday March 6, 2020, near the close of the day you go long, at a price near the settlement price of 41.57. Even though oil fell about 5 dollars a barrel that day, you feel good because all kinds of bullish events can happen to oil over weekends.

Except this weekend is different. Coronavirus (Covid-19) becomes much more newsworthy, and Russia and Saudi Arabia get into some kind of bizarre reverse price war over oil. On Sunday night, oil collapses and opens at 32.87, a drop of more than 20%, or $8,700 per contract.

You tell yourself "no more weekend" positions for me! This code helps you get out on weekends.

Plain English Rules
Close all positions at 4 PM Eastern on Friday. Do not allow any new trades, either.

Tradestation Code

```
//*********************************************
//
//www.kjtradingsystems.com
//Risk Protection Study
//Kevin Davey - Risk Protection #3 - No Weekends
//kdavey@kjtradingsystems.com
//
//*********************************************
//
input: lookback(10),stopATR(2),FridayStoptime(1600);
var:CanTrade(True);
```

```
CanTrade=True;
If dayofweek(date)=5 and time>=1600 then CanTrade=False;


If CanTrade=True then begin
If close crosses above close[lookback] and close crosses below
close[.5*lookback] then buy next bar at market;
If close crosses below close[lookback] and close crosses above
close[.5*lookback]  then sellshort next bar at market;


var:NewStop(3000);
NewStop=StopATR*AvgTrueRange(14)*BigPointValue;
If NewStop>3000 then NewStop=3000;

If StopATR<>0 then SetStopLoss(NewStop);



end;

If CanTrade=False then begin
Sell ("Friday-L Exit") next bar at market;
BuyToCover ("FridayL-S Exit") next bar at market;
end;
```

This will get you out of the market Friday afternoon, unless Friday is a holiday, a shortened holiday session or if you are using daily bars or a bar size that does not have a bar time ending at 1600. In those cases, you will have to make adjustments to the code.

This type of weekend exit can feel tremendous psychologically (imagine not having to worry about positions over the weekend!), but does it really help financially?

Results

Yikes!

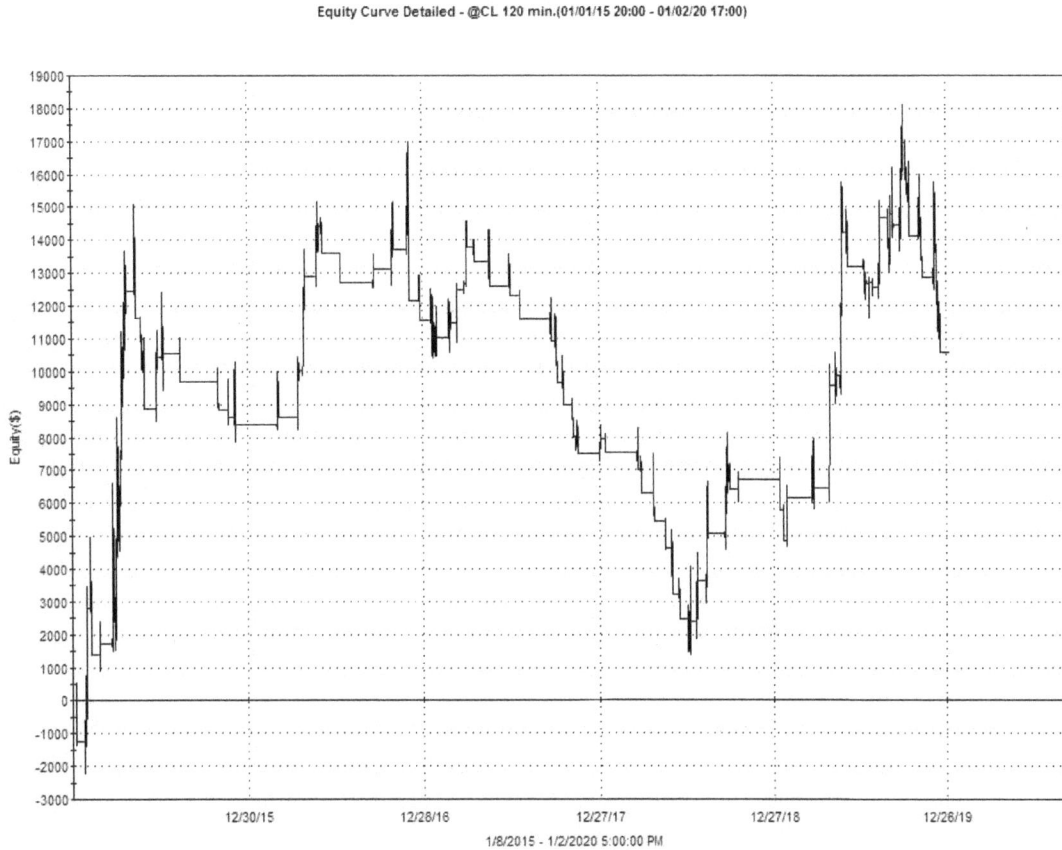

Equity Curve Detailed - @CL 120 min.(01/01/15 20:00 - 01/02/20 17:00)

Figure 26 - Closing All Trades Before Weekends

Exiting all trades before a weekend has a really negative impact on Crude Oil:

Performance Metric	Baseline Result	No Weekends (Exit at 4 PM Friday)
Net Profit	$40,030	$10,585
Number of Trades	92	107
Return On Account	280.7%	82.1%
Percent Time In Market	34.1%	8.2%
Max Drawdown (Closed Trade)	-$14,260	-$12,860

Figure 27- Impact Of No Weekends (Green/Light Gray is better)

The max drawdown is less, and the system is in the market a lot less

Volatility On/Off Switch of profits.   Clearly,   for   this

strategy/market, the "no weekend" trading idea is a financial loser.

Recommendation

This is a neat idea (who would not want stress free weekends?), but the benefit may be more psychological than financial. In fact, as we see with this particular strategy, it might be terrible financially.

But, as with all ideas, I recommend you test it, adding it to your strategy from the start. Don't create a strategy and then try to tack this on, since you'll only accept it if performance improves (which is cheating!).

Instead, if you like the idea, try it for a while during initial development. If you find yourself unable to create good strategies, then this weekend requirement might be the reason, and you might want to eliminate it.

Risk Protection #4 – If You Can't Stand The Heat, Get Out Of The Kitchen

Volatility is a double edged sword. As traders, we need volatility to profit from price movement. So some volatility is a good thing. But too much volatility can be a bad thing. It can mess up our algos, and trade us in and out of positions in an endless whipsaw.

Based on this concept I created code that would temporarily turn off strategies if volatility became too extreme. I shared it with a few traders and one trader showed me this before and after:

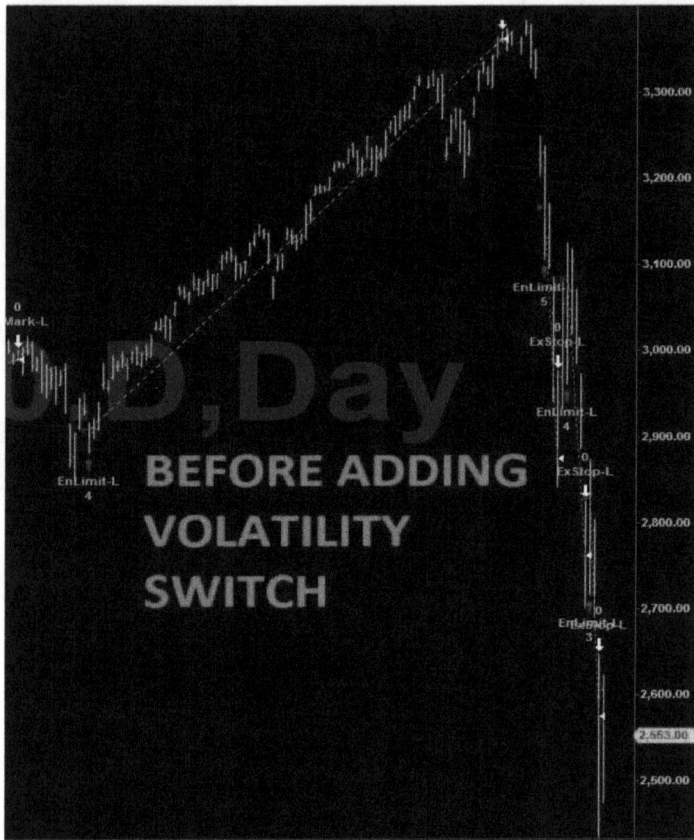

BEFORE ADDING VOLATILITY SWITCH

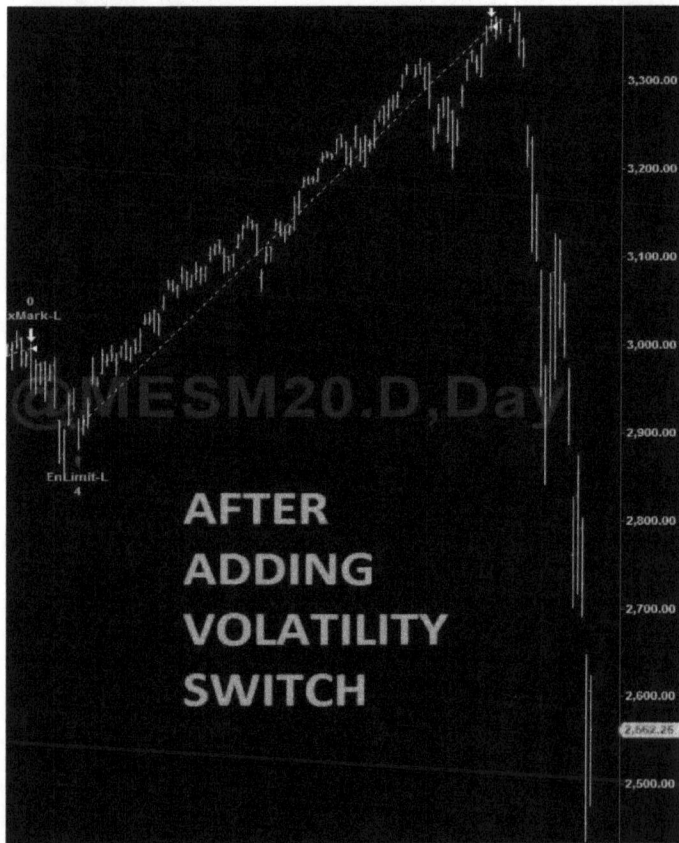

AFTER ADDING VOLATILITY SWITCH

Figure 28- Before and After Results, Volatility On/Off Switch

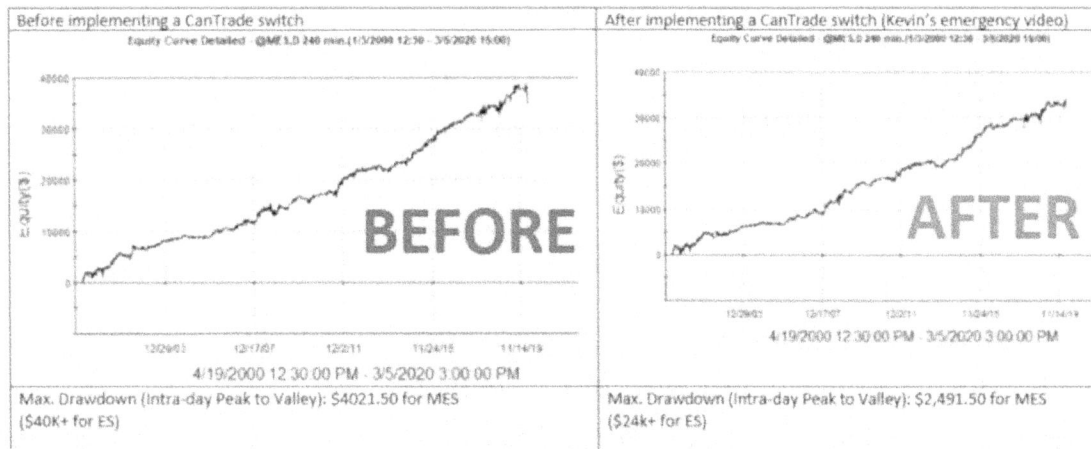

Figure 29- Before and After Equity Curves, Volatility On/Off Switch

So, at the very least, this high volatility kill switch is worth trying. Let's see how it works on the Crude Oil strategy.

Plain English Rules

Close all open trades, and do not allow any new trades, if the true range of the just closed bar is greater than ATRmult times the average true range over the last 5 bars.

Tradestation Code

```
//*******************************************
//
//www.kjtradingsystems.com
//Risk Protection Study
//Kevin Davey - Risk Protection #4 - High Volatility "Kill" Switch
//kdavey@kjtradingsystems.com
//
//*******************************************
//
input: lookback(10),stopATR(2),ATRMult(1600);
var:CanTrade(True);
```

```
//switch criteria
CANTRADE=TRUE;
If TrueRange>ATRMult*AvgTrueRange(5) then CANTRADE=FALSE;


If CanTrade=True then begin
If close crosses above close[lookback] and close crosses below
close[.5*lookback] then buy next bar at market;
If close crosses below close[lookback] and close crosses above
close[.5*lookback]  then sellshort next bar at market;


var:NewStop(3000);
NewStop=StopATR*AvgTrueRange(14)*BigPointValue;
If NewStop>3000 then NewStop=3000;

If StopATR<>0 then SetStopLoss(NewStop);



end;

If CanTrade=False then begin
Sell ("Vol-L Exit") next bar at market;
BuyToCover ("Vol-S Exit") next bar at market;
end;
```

Results

I optimized for different ATR multipliers, and the best case was better than the baseline case.

	KJD2020-03 RiskProtect 04: ATRMult	▲	Test	All: Net Profit	All: Total Trades	All: % Profitable
1	0		1	0.000	0	0.00
2	1		2	1,205.000	55	49.09
3	2		3	15,655.000	107	51.40
4	3		4	44,125.000	99	30.30
5	4		5	40,030.000	92	27.17
6	5		6	40,030.000	92	27.17

Figure 30 - Volatility Switch - Optimum Case Better Than Baseline

Performance Metric	Baseline Result	Kill Switch (optimized ATRMult=3)
Net Profit	$40,030	$44,125
Number of Trades	92	99
Return On Account	280.7%	319.1%
Percent Time In Market	34.1%	29.1
Max Drawdown (Closed Trade)	-$14,260	-$13,830

Figure 31 - Volatility Switch (Green/Light Gray is better)

But if the ATR multiplier is too small (meaning the kill switch is more active/sensitive), performance can quickly deteriorate. So, like anything else you optimize, it's a fine line between success and failure.

Recommendations

As with many of the other ideas presented so far, I'd treat the "kill" switch as a psychological enhancer, rather than a monetary performance enhancer.

This switch might not make your strategy more profitable, but you will be on the sidelines during periods of crazy volatility. That might be enough reason to use it.

Algo Trading Cheat Codes

* 4 unique ideas that can reduce the risk of an algo trading system:
1. Daily Loss Limiter
2. Entry Delay After Losing Trade

3. No Weekend Positions
4. High Volatility "Kill" Switch

* These 4 ideas can be used alone, or together, depending on your objectives
* Don't expect them to improve profit performance, but they may help improve your risk adjusted performance
* These techniques will help you psychologically, and that alone might make them worth doing
* If you want to add these to your strategy, remember:

A. Incorporate technique in the strategy, before testing (don't add these to already developed systems, since you'll likely only accept them if they improve performance, which is a form of optimizing)

B. Make sure to properly test and build the strategy (the Strategy Factory process is ideal for this)

C. Optimize these as little as possible. Try to select parameter values you feel comfortable with, rather than picking the best result from optimizing

CHAPTER 7 –
BULL/BEAR REGIME
TRADING

My wife Amy and I have different philosophies when it comes to parties. If the host says the party is from 6:00 PM to 11:00 PM, I like to be there at 6, and leave before 11. Amy, on the other hand, has no problem arriving at 7, and staying until midnight.

I worry I will miss something early, and she worries she'll miss some late night fun. Quite a pair we are! I thought about this recently in relation to algo trading, and market timing.

Everyone wants to hop on a bull trend right at the start, and ride it until it ends. When you look at a chart after the fact, it looks SO EASY. Just buy at the start, and sell at the end. Of course, you do the opposite for a bear trend. Piece of cake!!!

Figure 32 - Successfully Catching This Trend Is Easy - Right?

Market Wizard Dr. Van Tharp (whom I learned a lot from, and whom I usually agree with) breaks down markets into 3 phases:

- Bull Market
- Bear Market
- Flat Market

And within each market type, he defines 2 main characteristics:

- Volatile Market

- Non-Volatile Market

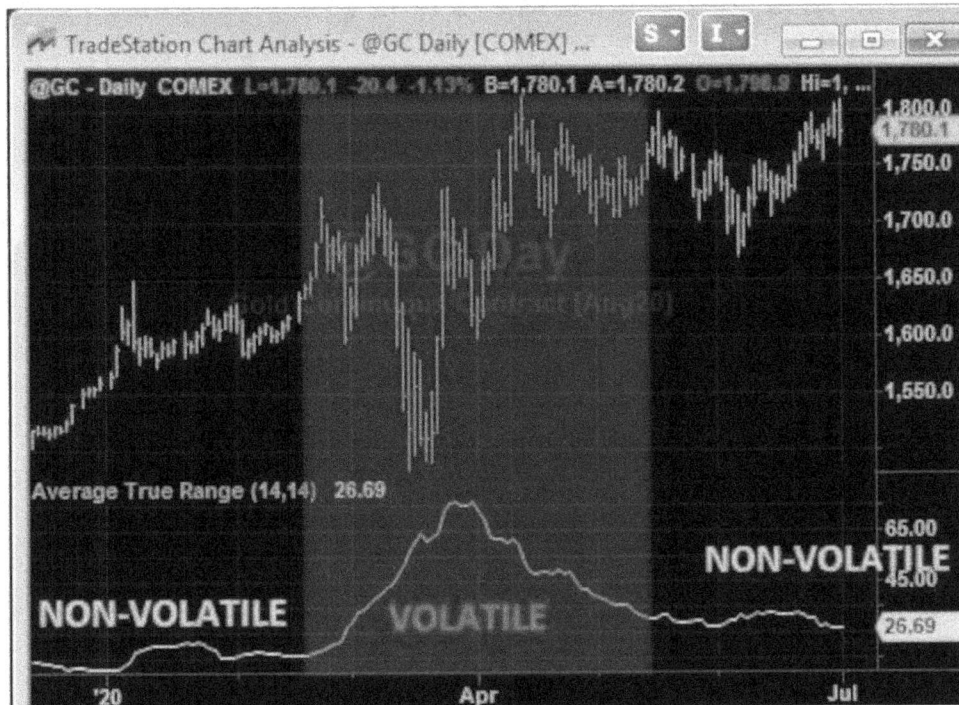

Figure 33 - Volatile and Non-Volatile Market Regimes

So, when you take all the combinations, you have 6 unique market types. Makes sense.

The theory behind all these market types is this:

Just find out what type of market you are in, and then simply trade a system that is best suited for that market. Sounds easy, doesn't it?

Sadly, reality (from what I've found) is not that simple. Referring back to my party story, it would be similar to getting a party invitation, but without a start or end time, or even a date. Arrive too early, and you'll be bored waiting for others. Arrive too late, and maybe most of the fun has already occurred before you got there!

Worst case, you miss the party completely - not a good thing. Same thing on the back end. Stay too long, or leave too early, and chances are you'll miss something entertaining.

Figure 34 - Are They Early Or Late To The Trend?

And that is where the bull/bear regime trading gets tricky. Successful market regime trading depends on having a solid regime identification plan/technique – in near real time.

Most traders can't do that, and that is where I disagree somewhat with Dr. Tharp that regime trading is fairly easy. My experience is that market regime timing, and turning on and off systems to match the current market, is very hard. Switching systems on and off requires a great switching mechanism, in addition to solid base strategies.

But maybe we can use the general idea of market regime, only with a single strategy, not a bunch of market regime specific strategies. Then all we need is a good base strategy, and a good regime detection approach.

With that in mind, let's see if a market regime project yields any useful results in this chapter.

Part 1- Bull, Bear and Flat Market Regime Trading

Part 2 – Bull and Bear, With Enhanced Flat Market Regime Trading

Part 3 – Volatile and Non-Volatile Regime Trading

Part 4 - Bull, Bear, Flat, Volatile and Non-Volatile Regimes, All 6 Combinations

Part 1 - Bull, Bear and Flat Market Regime Trading

The goal of this study is not to create a finalized, ready to trade strategy, but rather to do some research, and find out if taking only long trades in a bull market, and only short trades in a bear market, is something to consider.

If this approach proves worthwhile, then you could try it on existing strategies, new strategies, etc. In other words, you will have a LOT more testing to do! But that is a good thing - don't take my word for all this - test and verify it yourself - that is what good algo traders do.

Most traders, myself included, typically develop strategies that work in all market scenarios. We accept that sometimes our strategy will underperform in certain market periods, but overall it should be worthwhile to trade.

So why not create multiple strategies for each market? A bullish strategy for bull markets, a bearish one for bearish markets, and a "stay on the sidelines" strategy for flat markets?

I personally look at it like this. Let's say I develop one strategy with 2 optimized variables, over a 10 year period. "Mr. Market Timer" develops three (bull, bear, flat) strategies over that same period of time, each with 2 optimized variables. So, his chances of curvefitting or overfitting his models is at least 3 times higher than mine - after all, he is optimizing 3 strategies over the same time period I am optimizing just one.

I always think curvefitting is an evil best avoided, so minimizing variables and strategies is a very good idea.

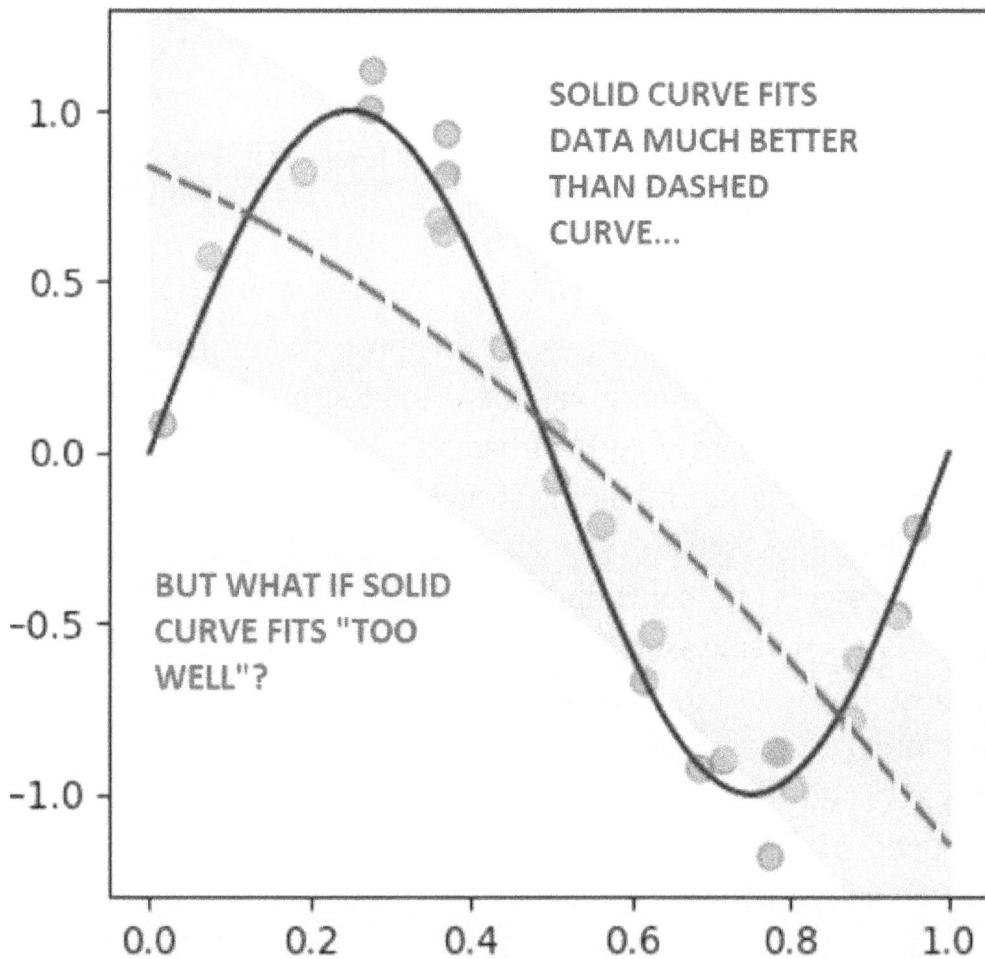

Figure 35 - Is Solid Curve A Better Model, Or Just Overfit?

In the figure above, there is no doubt that the solid curve better fits the data than the dashed curve. The solid curve is akin to a great looking backtest, compared to the dashed curve, a so-so looking backtest.

But what about the next few points of data, ones that are not shown on the curve? Which curve will be better at "predicting" those points? Before I started developing trading strategies, I'd say the solid curve was better. But after years and seeing (and sometimes creating) curvefitted algo trading systems, I'd now opt for the simpler dashed curve. Simple models work better in the future than more complicated models, at least in trading.

So, as I come into this study I am not a big personal fan of bull/bear regime trading - it adds complexity to trading models, and may cause more harm than good. Maybe I will change my mind as this study unfolds.

I'll keep an open mind regarding bull/bear regime trading, since after 30 years of trading, I've come to realize that the market does not care about my personal preferences. That is why I develop and evaluate every potential trading strategy I have. When the analysis is done properly, the numbers don't lie.

Core Strategies For This Study

I am going to use 4 core strategies for this project, and I'm also going to reverse the logic on each, which gives me 8 total strategies. These are just "test" strategies, not necessarily good or bad.

Strategy #1 is a simple breakout strategy. If the current close is the highest close of the last X bars, it buys at the open of the next bar with a market order. Vice versa for short trades.

Strategy #2 is a reverse simple breakout strategy. If the current close is the highest close of the last X bars, it sells short at the open of the next bar with a market order. Vice versa for long trades.

Strategy #3 is an RSI strategy. If the RSI is less than 30 (oversold), it buys at the open of the next bar with a market order. Short trades are signaled for RSI values above 70.

Strategy #4 is a reverse RSI strategy. If the RSI is less than 30 (oversold), it sells short at the open of the next bar with a market order. Long trades are signaled for RSI values above 70. Sample code for Tradestation is shown below.

```
// inputvar1 = 4 - RSI strategy
if  RSI (close, inputvar2)> 70 then buy next bar at market;
if  RSI (close, inputvar2) <30 then sellshort next bar at market;
```

Figure 36 - Test Strategy #4

Strategy #5 is a simple momentum strategy. If the current close is greater than the close X bars ago, it buys at the open of the next bar with a market order. Vice versa for short trades.

Strategy #6 is a reverse simple momentum strategy. If the current close is less than the close X bars ago, it buys at the open of the next bar with a market order. Vice versa for short trades.

Strategy #7 is a traditional moving average strategy. If the current close crosses above the average close of the last X bars, it buys at the open of the next bar with a market order. Vice versa for short trades.

Strategy #8 is a reverse traditional moving average strategy. If the current close crosses below the average close of the last X bars, it buys at the open of the next bar with a market order. Vice versa for short trades.

Note that each of these core strategies is a pretty common approach to trading. I chose them because they were simple and fairly well known. Each of these strategies has a single parameter than can be optimized – the lookback length X. I will use 10, 30 or 50 bars for this optimization.

Bull/Bear/Flat Filters For This Study

There are a ton of different bull/bear filters I could have tried here. I chose 6 (one is "always trading").

Filter #1 – "Always" Trade Filter. Allow long and short trades with no restrictions.

Filter #2 – Moving Average Filter. Only allow long trades when the current close is above the average close over the last InputVar4 bars. Vice versa for short trades. This is a bull or bear filter. Tradestation code is shown below as an example.

```
CanTradeLong = False;
CanTradeShort = False;
If close> average (close, InputVar4) Then CanTradeLong = True;
If close <average (close, InputVar4) Then CanTradeShort = True;
```

Figure 37 - Sample Filter

Filter #3 – Momentum Filter. Only allow long trades when the current close is above close InputVar4 bars ago. Vice versa for short trades. This is a bull or bear filter.

Filter #4 – High Or Low First Filter. Over the last InputVar4 bars, did the highest high occur more recently than the lowest low? If so, take only long trades. Vice versa for short trades. This is a bull or bear filter.

Filter #5 – ADX Filter. Only allow trades when the InputVar4 bar ADX is above 15. This value suggests at least a weak trend is in place. Below 15 for the ADX, just remain flat. This is a flat or not flat filter.

Filter #6 – RSI Filter. If the RSI over the last InputVar4 bars is below 70, only allow long trades. If the RSI over the last InputVar4 bars is above 30, only allow short trades. This is a bull or bear filter.

As you can see, most of the filters break down the market action into a bull market or a bear market. In part 2, I'll take one of these filters and add specific flat regimes to it.

I will be trying different values of InputVar4 for this study. Since the core strategy signals themselves are using short term lengths of 10-50, for the filters I will use longer lengths for InputVar4 of 100, 150 and 200.

Markets and Bar Sizes For This Study

I will be examining 40 different continuous contract futures markets:

@AD, @BO, @BP, @C, @CC, @CD, @CL, @CT, @DX, @EC, @EMD, @ES, @FC, @FV, @GC, @HG, @HO , @JY, @KC, @KW, @LC, @LH, @NG, @NK, @NQ, @O, @OJ, @PL, @RB, @RR, @S, @SB, @SF, @SI, @SM, @RTY, @TY, @US, @W, @YM

I will also be using 5 bar sizes:
Daily, 720 minute, 360 minute, 120 minute and 60 minute bars

Other Study Info

This will be a 10 year study, from Jan 2009 to Dec 2018.

All results shown are for 1 contract, and include appropriate slippage and commission specific to each market. (If you did not realize, each market has its own characteristic slippage, based on its volume, liquidity, contract size, etc.)

All together, we then have:
40 markets
5 bar sizes
8 strategies
3 values for length X for each strategy

6 bull/bear filters

3 values for length InputVar4 for each filter

This will produce 86,400 unique backtests. You might say – this will take a long time to complete, as it is a big study with many markets and bar sizes. How can you do this in a timely fashion?

Well, to help me out, I will be using Multi-Opt, a special software tool created specifically for Tradestation. It is available only to my Strategy Factory workshop students, and in fact was written by a longtime student. This software allows for rapid testing and prototyping of strategies - just one of many timesaving tasks it performs.

Multi-Opt is going to be my virtual assistant on this project. Otherwise this study would take days or weeks! With Multi-Opt, Tradestation 9.5 and a 2 year old laptop, each part of the study takes about 7 hours to run.

Results

First, here is an example of what a filter does to the strategy. The top chart contains the strategy with no trend regime filter – it can go long or short at any time, without restrictions.

In the bottom chart, there is a trend regime filter based on momentum. When the 100 bar momentum is up (shown with light blue/white bars), only long trades can be taken. When the momentum is down (shown with red/dark gray bars), only short trades are permitted.

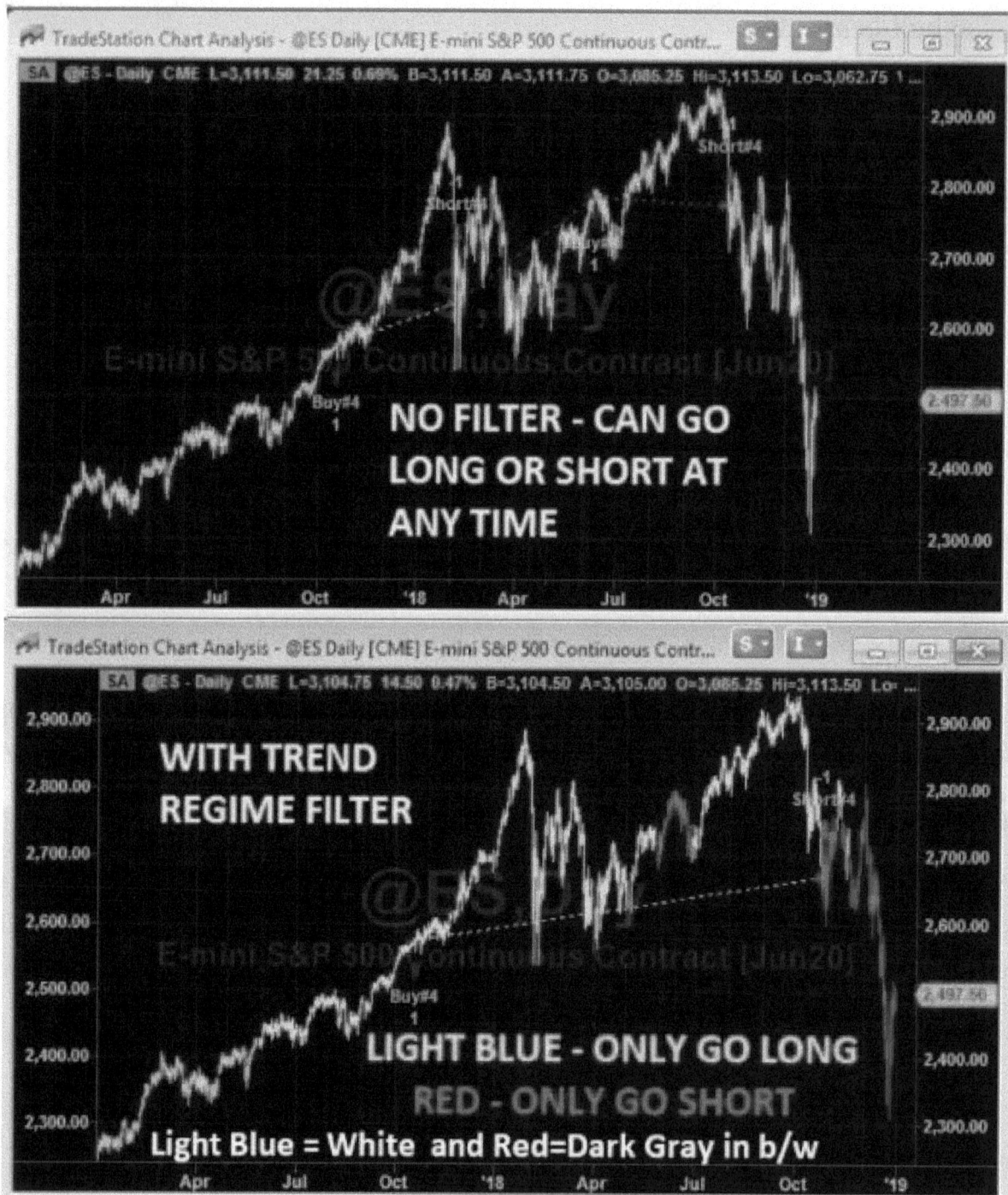

Figure 38- Trades With and Without Regime Filter

With so many markets, bar sizes, etc, it is clear that just analyzing the results can be overwhelming. So, I am only looking at 2 performance metrics:

Overall Net Profit

Maximum Intraday Drawdown

I obviously could have chosen a ton of various metrics, but one metric for profit and one for risk should tell me what I want to know.

With that, let's get started with analyzing the results.

First, let's take a look at the impact of the Regime Filter:

Row Labels ▾	Average of Net Profit	Average of Max Intraday Drawdown
filter 1	($50,518.1)	($79,423.5)
filter 2	($8,058.1)	($37,805.3)
filter 3	($7,154.2)	($38,043.1)
filter 4	($6,935.8)	($38,529.1)
filter 5	($3,866.9)	($31,214.8)
filter 6	($50,523.0)	($79,434.9)
Grand Total	($21,176.0)	($50,741.8)

Figure 39 - Results With Regime Filters

At first glance, it appears like nothing works. No matter what filter is used, on average the strategies all lose money. But, a second glance reveals some interesting results:

Filter #1 is the baseline, which is no filter at all – all trades were taken. It is pretty bad overall.

Filters #2 thru #5 show a pretty dramatic improvement in average Net Profit compared to the baseline, and also a significant reduction in maximum drawdown. This shows that the filters appear to work, at least in some situations.

Filter #6 shows basically no change from the baseline. I am guessing it is not doing much if any filtering at all.

Maybe though, the averages are deceiving, and possibly skewed by a few strategies. Let's take a look at the results for each strategy:

Row Labels	Average of Net Profit	Average of Max Intraday Drawdown		Net Profit Improvement Over Filter #1 (Baseline)	Max Drawdown Improvement Over Filter #1 (Baseline)
⊟strat 1	-13351.5	-44834.6			
filter 1	-26576.5	-58354.0			
filter 2	-10282.6	-41782.2		16,293.88	16,571.79
filter 3	-6666.9	-39409.3		19,909.63	18,944.70
filter 4	-6412.1	-39434.3		20,164.46	18,919.74
filter 5	-3548.4	-31630.5		23,028.10	26,723.53
filter 6	-26622.5	-58397.5		(46.01)	(43.48)
⊟strat 2	-14685.5	-49330.3			
filter 1	-33727.0	-69019.7			
filter 2	-5490.5	-39253.7		28,236.51	29,766.01
filter 3	-6123.8	-41512.0		27,603.23	27,507.66
filter 4	-7965.4	-43929.9		25,761.59	25,089.83
filter 5	-1095.3	-33258.8		32,631.68	35,760.92
filter 6	-33711.0	-69007.8		16.00	11.91
⊟strat 3	-1022.1	-26352.2			
filter 1	-2217.4	-41843.2			
filter 2	-1082.5	-12647.2		1,134.82	29,195.96
filter 3	-1003.9	-18280.1		1,213.44	23,563.07
filter 4	-1619.5	-20431.5		597.81	21,411.69
filter 5	2024.7	-23066.6		4,242.02	18,776.53
filter 6	-2234.0	-41844.8		(16.62)	(1.67)
⊟strat 4	-5591.9	-32923.3			
filter 1	-7067.6	-36319.7			
filter 2	-6541.1	-35246.4		526.47	1,073.39
filter 3	-5015.7	-34219.5		2,051.94	2,100.25
filter 4	-5048.4	-33919.3		2,019.16	2,400.44
filter 5	-2809.1	-21520.4		4,258.45	14,799.32
filter 6	-7069.5	-36314.4		(1.92)	5.31

⊟ strat 5	-28061.0	-56691.8		
filter 1	-66131.9	-90920.5		
filter 2	-13152.1	-43144.3	52,979.85	47,776.11
filter 3	-9414.3	-40954.7	56,717.63	49,965.75
filter 4	-6814.8	-40161.7	59,317.10	50,758.79
filter 5	-6760.3	-34046.6	59,371.63	56,873.83
filter 6	-66092.4	-90923.1	39.53	(2.64)
⊟ strat 6	-33977.6	-64795.1		
filter 1	-84485.6	-109349.3		
filter 2	-9181.9	-44021.1	75,303.73	65,328.17
filter 3	-11143.0	-44903.7	73,342.58	64,445.53
filter 4	-9460.6	-44552.2	75,025.01	64,797.04
filter 5	-5099.3	-36565.3	79,386.32	72,783.96
filter 6	-84495.6	-109378.7	(9.99)	(29.41)
⊟ strat 7	-32456.2	-61997.1		
filter 1	-81330.1	-105436.4		
filter 2	-8775.1	-43272.6	72,554.97	62,163.82
filter 3	-8505.8	-42365.0	72,824.31	63,071.49
filter 4	-8352.6	-42560.0	72,977.54	62,876.44
filter 5	-6426.1	-32881.8	74,904.03	72,554.68
filter 6	-81347.5	-105466.6	(17.44)	(30.21)
⊟ strat 8	-40262.3	-69010.0		
filter 1	-102608.7	-124145.3		
filter 2	-9959.1	-43075.2	92,649.61	81,070.13
filter 3	-9360.2	-42700.2	93,248.55	81,445.08
filter 4	-9813.1	-43244.3	92,795.64	80,901.03
filter 5	-7221.2	-36748.5	95,387.46	87,396.81
filter 6	-102611.3	-124146.5	(2.64)	(1.26)

Figure 40 - Results By Strategy

Lots of data here, so just focus on the 2 far right columns. Black numbers show that the regime filter is better than the baseline "always trade" case. Red/gray (negative) numbers show regime trading is worse.

The results are clear – filters #2 - #5 all improve Net Profit and Max Drawdown, for each of the 8 strategies. Sometimes the impact is small (for example with Strategy #4), and other times it is dramatic (for example with strategy #8).

This tells us that bull/bear regime filtering is a good idea! Using filters #2, #3 and #4, only take long trends when the long term trend indicator is indicating a bull market. Use filter #5 as a general trend / no trend indicator.

What is surprising is that it does not matter much which filter is used – their results are all more or less the same. Maybe these particular filters all catch the same big trends?

What about the lookback length of the filter, which in the test was set from 100-200 bars? Does this variable play a role?

Again, a lot of data in the table below - just focus on the green highlighted cells.

Average of Net Profit	Column Label				Average of Max Intraday Drawdown	Column Labels			
Row Labels	big L 100	big L 150	big L 200	Grand Total	Row Labels	big L 100	big L 150	big L 200	Grand Total
strat 1	-15038.6	-12641.9	-12374.0	-13351.5	strat 1	-47352.6	-44573.4	-42577.9	-44834.6
filter 2	-11437.4	-9747.5	-9865.0	-10282.6	filter 2	-44158.0	-40784.6	-40404.1	-41782.2
filter 3	-9558.0	-4902.5	-5540.2	-6666.9	filter 3	-41022.6	-38814.7	-38390.6	-39409.3
filter 4	-8226.2	-6249.7	-4760.3	-6412.1	filter 4	-40759.2	-39506.7	-38087.0	-39434.3
filter 5	-7810.5	-1693.9	-1140.8	-3548.4	filter 5	-41451.0	-31544.7	-21895.8	-31630.5
strat 2	-15103.8	-14643.5	-14309.1	-14685.5	strat 2	-51517.5	-49144.8	-47328.6	-49330.3
filter 2	-5159.1	-5552.0	-5760.3	-5490.5	filter 2	-39430.3	-38964.9	-39365.8	-39253.7
filter 3	-6794.8	-5357.1	-6219.4	-6123.8	filter 3	-42868.2	-41119.4	-40548.4	-41512.0
filter 4	-10101.0	-7646.2	-6149.0	-7965.4	filter 4	-46793.4	-43338.6	-41657.5	-43929.9
filter 5	-1117.5	-1831.1	-327.1	-1095.3	filter 5	-41991.4	-33400.2	-24384.7	-33258.8
strat 3	-940.8	-1064.2	-1061.4	-1022.1	strat 3	-27128.5	-26302.2	-25625.9	-26352.2
filter 2	518.1	-1164.4	-1565.1	-1082.5	filter 2	-12134.8	-12767.2	-13039.6	-12647.2
filter 3	-1788.6	-1215.7	7.4	-1003.9	filter 3	-16406.5	-18736.5	-19697.3	-18280.1
filter 4	-1717.0	-2852.5	789.1	-1619.5	filter 4	-17747.5	-21205.1	-22343.8	-20431.5
filter 5	2870.0	2788.0	416.0	2024.7	filter 5	-22774.8	-21421.3	-15004.0	-23066.6
strat 4	-6180.0	-5459.4	-5136.3	-5591.9	strat 4	-34330.8	-33066.5	-31372.6	-32923.3
filter 2	-6863.4	-6509.2	-6250.8	-6541.1	filter 2	-35707.9	-35183.4	-34847.7	-35246.4
filter 3	-6018.0	-4159.3	-4869.7	-5015.7	filter 3	-34610.8	-33999.9	-34047.8	-34219.5
filter 4	-5591.5	-4714.3	-4779.6	-5048.4	filter 4	-34076.5	-34067.2	-33614.1	-33919.3
filter 5	-4430.9	-3225.3	-2712.2	-2809.1	filter 5	-28922.5	-22562.8	-18076.0	-21520.4
strat 5	-30676.8	-27039.4	-26466.8	-28061.0	strat 5	-59858.8	-56097.0	-54119.6	-56691.8
filter 2	-15807.8	-12543.5	-11105.0	-13152.1	filter 2	-46487.9	-42101.1	-40844.0	-43144.3
filter 3	-13599.0	-6220.8	-8423.0	-9414.3	filter 3	-43424.6	-39411.8	-40027.7	-40954.7
filter 4	-8791.3	-6583.5	-5069.7	-6814.8	filter 4	-41532.6	-39483.1	-39459.3	-40161.7
filter 5	-13591.4	-4633.4	-2656.0	-6760.3	filter 5	-45827.6	-33756.9	-22555.4	-34046.6
strat 6	-35562.8	-33654.3	-32715.9	-33977.6	strat 6	-67627.6	-64365.7	-62391.9	-64795.1
filter 2	-10000.7	-9473.2	-8071.1	-9181.9	filter 2	-45390.2	-44073.1	-42600.0	-44021.1
filter 3	-14216.9	-8846.5	-10365.3	-11143.0	filter 3	-47844.3	-43370.3	-43496.6	-44903.7
filter 4	-11549.3	-9979.9	-6852.5	-9460.6	filter 4	-46494.1	-44205.0	-42957.6	-44552.2
filter 5	-8701.6	-4581.7	-2014.5	-5099.3	filter 5	-47334.5	-35776.0	-26585.4	-36565.3
strat 7	-34312.6	-31605.8	-31450.2	-32456.2	strat 7	-64859.1	-61532.4	-59599.7	-61997.1
filter 2	-10541.0	-8240.2	-7544.2	-8775.1	filter 2	-45613.5	-42701.1	-41503.8	-43272.6
filter 3	-10828.1	-5245.3	-9444.0	-8505.8	filter 3	-44606.9	-40592.1	-41895.9	-42365.0
filter 4	-10097.9	-8215.6	-6744.1	-8352.6	filter 4	-43727.9	-42444.4	-41507.7	-42560.0
filter 5	-11748.8	-5235.3	-2294.1	-6426.1	filter 5	-44321.0	-32542.2	-21782.1	-32881.8
strat 8	-42721.9	-39387.1	-38677.8	-40262.3	strat 8	-72252.3	-68384.7	-66392.9	-69010.0
filter 2	-12076.2	-9672.2	-8128.9	-9959.1	filter 2	-45230.4	-42503.3	-41491.7	-43075.2
filter 3	-12018.5	-7033.1	-9028.6	-9360.2	filter 3	-44835.3	-41051.5	-42213.8	-42700.2
filter 4	-13551.5	-8825.3	-7062.4	-9813.1	filter 4	-45562.3	-42893.1	-41277.4	-43244.3
filter 5	-13453.7	-5576.8	-2655.3	-7221.2	filter 5	-49599.6	-35544.5	-25181.3	-36748.5
Grand Total	-22567.2	-20687.0	-20273.9	-21176.0	Grand Total	-53115.9	-50433.3	-48676.2	-50741.8

Figure 41- Highlighted Results Show Better Performance

The green highlighted cells are the highest net profit and lowest drawdown for every row. A quick glance shows that in a majority of cases, the lookback length of 200 is the best - those are the columns with the most green cells. This length of 200 bars corresponds to the longest time period to measure the trend.

Note that it is not 200 "days" except for daily bars. For a 60 minute chart, use 200 of the 60 minute bars.

What Conclusions Can We Draw So Far?

With so many markets, bar sizes, etc. there are many ways to dissect this data. But for this study I'd like to keep it general.

The general conclusions thus far are:

- Trend Based Bull/Bear Regime Filters On Average Improve Net Profit, And Reduce Drawdown
- For Filters That Work, There Is Not A Large Degree Of Variation Between Best Filters and Worst Filters
- The Longer The Regime Filter Lookback Length, The Better The Results

So, if I was to incorporate a bull/bear trend filter in my own testing, I would code something like this (using Momentum filter #3):

```
Variables: CanTradeLong(False), CanTradeShort(False);
CanTradeLong = False;
CanTradeShort = False;
If close> close [200] Then CanTradeLong = True;
If close <close [200] Then CanTradeShort = True;

if CanTradeLong = True and {my long entry rule}  then buy next bar at market;
if CanTradeShort = True and {my short entry rule}  then sellshort next bar at market;
```

A Small Inspiration For You

Just as an example of the possible improvement with a trend regime filter, here is strategy #4 with 120 minute Silver bars, with and without the trend filter #3 incorporated.

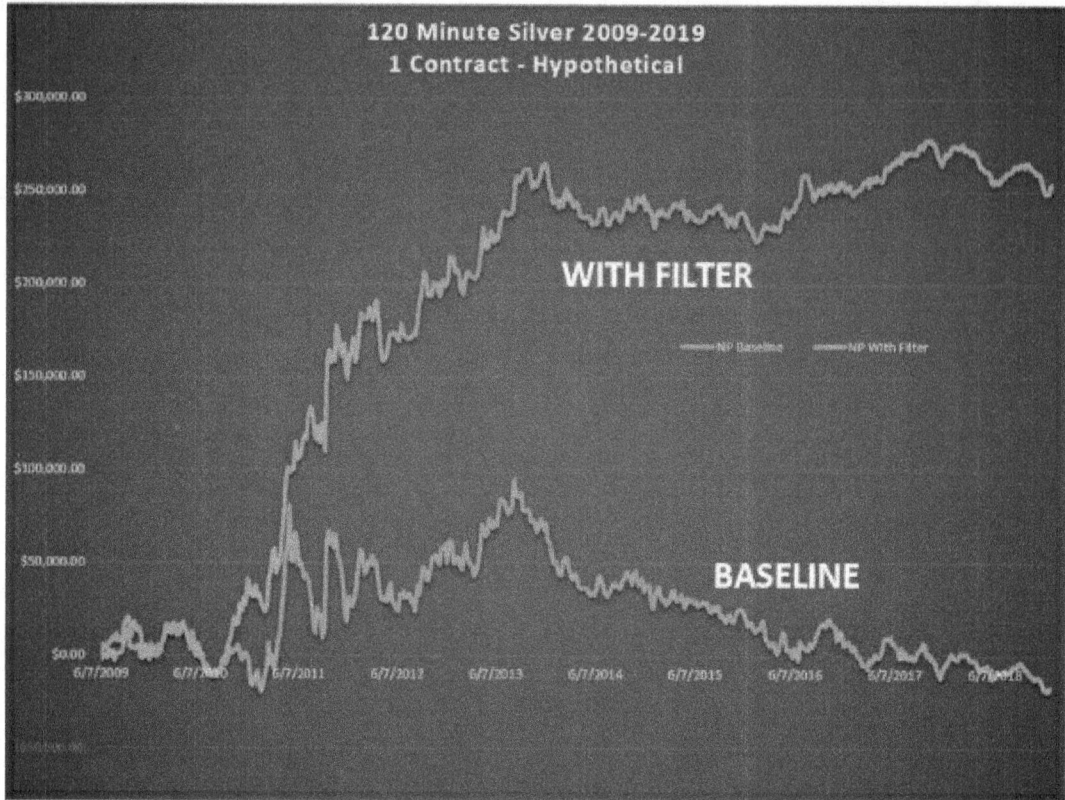

Figure 42 - Possible Improvement With Regime Filtering

Quite a difference! After doing this initial study, a few lingering questions still bothered me a bit. What is the impact of instead of just bull/bear regimes, adding in a flat regime, to make it bull/bear/flat? Also, Filter #6 (RSI filter) did nothing – why?

Those questions will be discussed below.

Part 2 - Expanded Bull, Bear and Flat Market Regime Trading

For Part 2, I am going to dig a bit more into regime filtering. Specifically, I am going to see if adding a "flat" period excluder to an existing filter is of any help. The idea here is that you do not initiate new trades during a defined flat period. It could also mean that during a flat period existing trades will be exited (I will try both versions).

The second topic I wanted to examine was the RSI trend filter. In Part 1, I found that this filter – filter #6 – did nothing. This needs to be examined further.

So first I will tackle the second topic. In Part 1, I had filter #6 - a simple RSI filter. It did pretty much nothing – why?

Here is its definition:

Filter #6 – RSI Filter. If the RSI over the last Y bars is below 70, only allow long trades. If the RSI over the last Y bars is above 30, only allow short trades. This is a bull or bear filter.

When I added this, I really did not look too much into it, I just used fairly loose overbought and oversold levels of 30 and 70, figuring it would work.

Not so fast my friend!

Turns out when you calculate RSI over 100-200 bars, the value rarely, if ever, gets above 70 or below 30. Here is an example:

Figure 43 - RSI of 100-200 Bars Rarely Goes Above 70 / Below

So, that explains why this filter is useless. And the bad part is for the Part 2 study, I originally used RSI variations like this for new Filters #5 and #6. And they either do no filtering, or complete filtering (no trades at all!).

As a result, I am going to eliminate RSI from trend filtering. I could probably play around with it, and get it to work, but I am always wary of trying to make something work. For me, trying too hard usually leads to curvefitting and overfitting.

In Part 1, the moving average Filter (#2), the momentum Filter (#3), the High Or Low First Filter (#4) and the ADX Filter (#5) all did reasonably well, with the ADX filter being the best.

For this part of the study, I am going to use the momentum filter #3, which was in the middle of the pack on filter performance.

Why not just use the best (ADX #5) filter? Well, remember the goal here is not to find the best filter for trends, but rather to just see how the concept works in general across many markets and bar sizes. I think using an average performing filter can give me more insight into future performance. Of course, I could be wrong on that!

With that, let's look at candidate filters for the Part 2 study. We will have 4 filters, which I'll identify as "Mome" filters for "momentum:"

Mome Filter #1 – "Always" Trade Filter. Allow long and short trades with no restrictions. This should equal (or be very close to) Filter #1 in Part 1.

Mome Filter #2 – Momentum Filter. Only allow long trades when the current close is above close Y bars ago. Vice versa for short trades. This is a bull or bear filter. This should equal (or be very close to) Filter #3 in Part 1.

Mome Filter #3 – Momentum Filter II. Only allow long trades when the current close is above close Y bars ago AND if the current close is above the close Y/2 bars ago. Vice versa for short trades. This filter will be flat whenever there is conflicting short and long period momentum.

Mome Filter #4 – ADX Filter. Only allow long trades when the current close is above close Y bars ago AND if the ADX is above 15 (signifying trend mode). Vice versa for short trades. This filter will be flat when the

ADX is flat.

An example of the 4 cases is shown in the figures below. This provides an idea of how selective these filters are.

@GC - 60 min COMEX L=1,795.5 5.5 0.31% B=1,795.4 A=1,795.6 O=1,787.0 Hi=1,797.6 Lo=1,779.2 ...

Mome Filter #1

KJD2020-06 2Regimes () 1.00 -1.00

When Yellow line=1, can trade long

When Light Blue line=-1, can trade short

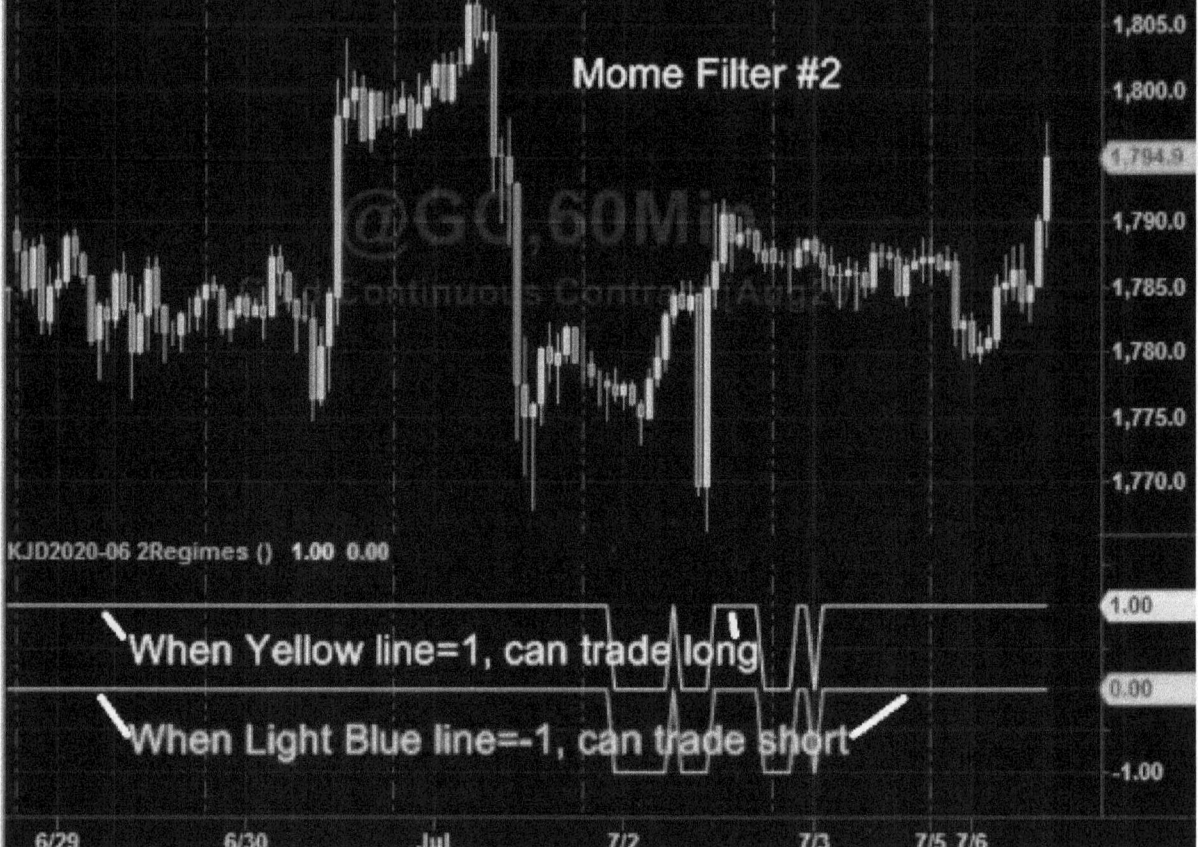

Mome Filter #2

@GC - 60 min COMEX L=1,794.8 4.8 0.27% B=1,794.7 A=1,794.8 O=1,787.0 Hi=1,797.6 Lo=1,779.2 ...

Mome Filter #3

KJD2020-06 2Regimes () 0.00 0.00

When Yellow line=1, can trade long

When Light Blue line=-1, can trade short

Figure 44- Momentum Filters

Here are the results for different momentum filters.

Row Labels	Average of Net Profit	Average of Max Intraday Drawdown
mome filter 1 -None	($50,480.5)	($79,404.0)
mome filter 2	($7,151.5)	($38,053.8)
mome filter 3	($5,589.3)	($35,067.9)
mome filter 4	($4,217.7)	($25,337.8)
Grand Total	($16,859.8)	($44,465.9)

Figure 45- Impact of Momentum Filters

Momentum 3 and 4 filters (with "flat" periods as opposed to only bull and bear periods) do perform better. Both the net profit and max drawdown improved by about 60%. That is pretty good performance improvement.

When the results are examined across all 8 of the core strategies, the filters improve each strategy. Sometimes the difference is small, and sometimes it is very large.

Row Labels	Average of Net Profit	Average of Max Intraday Drawdown	Net Profit Improvement Over Filter #1 (Baseline)	Max Drawdown Improvement Over Filter #1 (Baseline)
⊟ strat 1				
mome filter 1 -None	-26617.0	-58402.9		
mome filter 2	-6651.0	-39470.4	$19,966	$18,933
mome filter 3	-4765.3	-37724.5	$21,852	$20,678
mome filter 4	-5039.3	-28931.1	$21,578	$29,472
⊟ strat 2				
mome filter 1 -None	-33661.6	-68966.3		
mome filter 2	-6136.1	-41529.7	$27,525	$27,437
mome filter 3	-4728.4	-38702.2	$28,933	$30,264
mome filter 4	-4277.2	-27774.6	$29,384	$41,192
⊟ strat 3				
mome filter 1 -None	-2240.1	-41842.3		
mome filter 2	-1007.5	-18324.4	$1,233	$23,518
mome filter 3	-1510.0	-13351.3	$730	$28,491
mome filter 4	-1356.8	-9661.0	$883	$32,181
⊟ strat 4				
mome filter 1 -None	-7055.6	-36297.6		
mome filter 2	-4991.4	-34219.6	$2,064	$2,078
mome filter 3	-4563.9	-33690.2	$2,492	$2,607
mome filter 4	-3254.2	-20425.3	$3,801	$15,872
⊟ strat 5				
mome filter 1 -None	-66103.7	-90980.6		
mome filter 2	-9311.9	-40915.6	$56,792	$50,065
mome filter 3	-6068.2	-38284.4	$60,035	$52,696
mome filter 4	-5277.5	-30404.7	$60,826	$60,576
⊟ strat 6				
mome filter 1 -None	-84369.5	-109263.4		
mome filter 2	-11203.0	-44926.3	$73,166	$64,337
mome filter 3	-6753.2	-36761.0	$77,616	$72,502
mome filter 4	-4802.2	-29322.7	$79,567	$79,941
⊟ strat 7				
mome filter 1 -None	-81252.5	-105399.3		
mome filter 2	-8566.4	-42382.6	$72,686	$63,017
mome filter 3	-8361.2	-41275.0	$72,891	$64,124
mome filter 4	-4749.8	-27627.2	$76,503	$77,772
⊟ strat 8				
mome filter 1 -None	-102544.4	-124079.7		
mome filter 2	-9345.0	-42662.0	$93,199	$81,418
mome filter 3	-7963.8	-40754.9	$94,581	$83,325
mome filter 4	-4984.6	-28555.5	$97,560	$95,524
Grand Total	-16859.8	-44465.9		

Figure 46- Momentum Filters For All Strategies

Digging a little deeper, the impact of the various filter can best be seen with the average number of trades. Compared to no filter (Mome Filter #1), many of the trades get filtered out with Mome Filter #4. An example of that is shown below.

With no trades filtered out, this strategy has 1153 trades. Quite a few!

Equity Curve Line - @RB 60 min.(1/1/2009 19:00 - 12/31/2018 17:00)

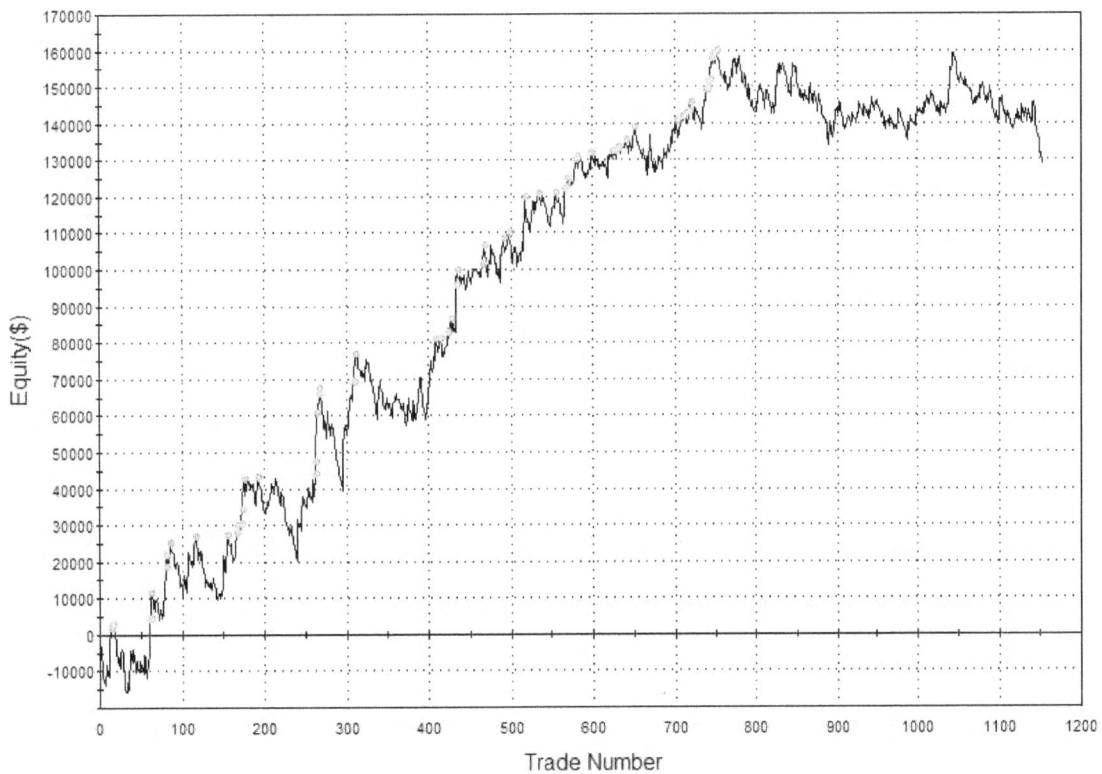

Figure 47- No Trades Filtered Out

Once trades are filtered out with Mome Filter #4, the number of trades drops to only 18:

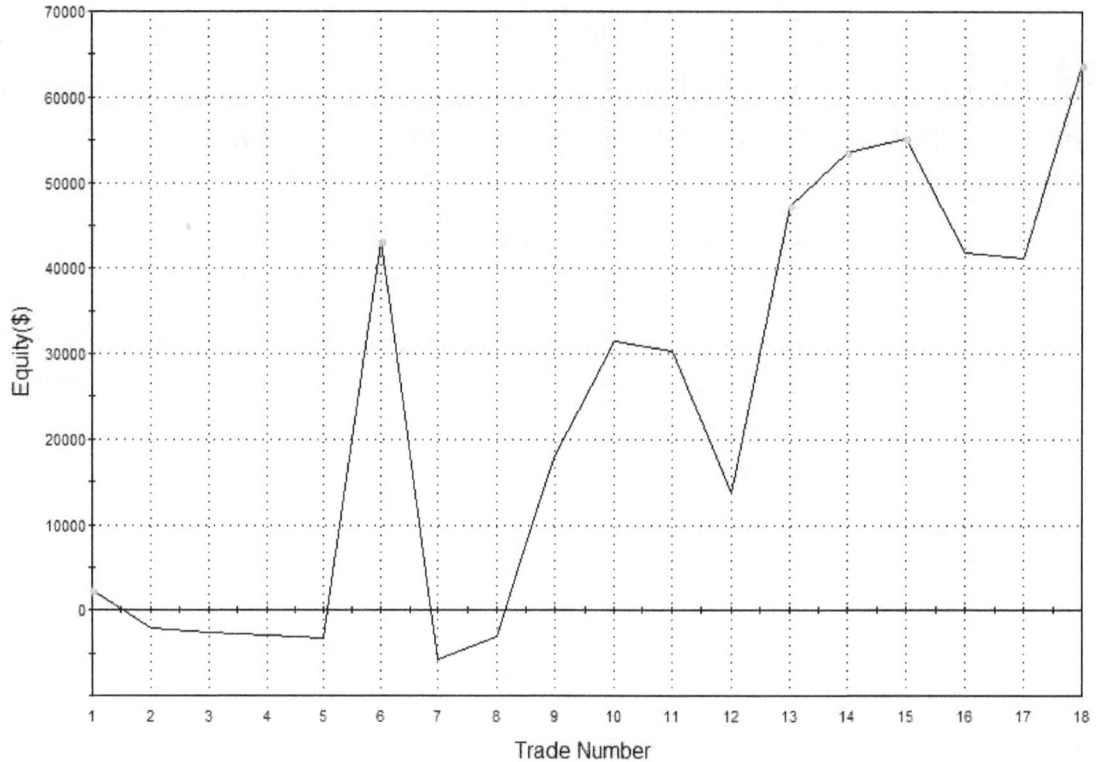

Figure 48- With Trades Filtered Out

This is pretty typical. The filters remove many trades, especially for "mome filter #4."

Row Labels	Average of Total Trades
mome filter 1 -None	1071.5
mome filter 2	139.2
mome filter 3	93.2
mome filter 4	9.0
Grand Total	328.2

Figure 49- Impact Of Filter On Number Of Trades

So, while it is nice in general to have more trades, all other things being equal, filtering can reduce the number of bad trades, making the performance better on average. Of course, you have to watch out for "over filtering!"

Some of these filters remove too many trades. Beware of that - a small number of trades - when doing any testing. Statistically inclined traders would likely cringe when the number of trades goes below 50 or so. The smaller the number of trades, the less reliable the results will be.

Overall Results

I was a bit surprised that adding a "flat" period to the bull/bear regime did not improve results by that much. There was quite a bit of improvement with Mome filter #4, but the very small number of trades gives me pause. I'd be inclined to use Mome filter #3, as it reduces the number of trades but also keeps many of them.

I should point out that I was "always in" the market, even with the flat filter. Here is an explanation:

Bull market – can only initiate long trades, simultaneously exiting the short trade

Bear market – can only initiate short trades, simultaneously exiting the long trade

Flat market – cannot exit or enter trades during the flat period

This approach does not keep from being in trades during flat periods; it just restricts new trades during flat periods. That is sort of "half flat!"

As a result, I decided to run the cases again, adding the appropriate code for each strategy.

NEW FILTER

Row Labels	Average of Net Profit	Average of Max Intraday Drawdown
mome bbf filter 1 -None	($50,480.4)	($79,403.9)
mome bbf filter 2	($7,461.5)	($37,288.9)
mome bbf filter 3	($10,235.8)	($27,321.5)
mome bbf filter 4	($1,872.1)	($7,737.1)

ORIGINAL FILTER

Row Labels	Average of Net Profit	Average of Max Intraday Drawdown
mome filter 1 -None	($50,480.5)	($79,404.0)
mome filter 2	($7,151.5)	($38,053.8)
mome filter 3	($5,589.3)	($35,067.9)
mome filter 4	($4,217.7)	($25,337.8)
Grand Total	($16,859.8)	($44,465.9)

Figure 50- Comparison Of Old And New Filters

Results for filter #2 are pretty much the same, filter #3 is mixed (lower profit, but also lower drawdown) and filter #4 is better (but again, filter #4 does not have many trades). So, nothing definitive here – it seems to be dependent on the filter, instead of being universally good or bad.

Conclusion of Part 2

When we look at net profit, both filters #4 are best.

Filter	profit	drawdown	trades
mome bbf filter 4	(1,872)	(7,737)	14
mome filter 4	(4,218)	(25,338)	9
mome filter 3	(5,589)	(35,068)	93
mome filter 2	(7,152)	(38,054)	139
mome bbf filter 2	(7,461)	(37,289)	155
mome bbf filter 3	(10,236)	(27,321)	259
mome bbf filter 1 -None	(50,480)	(79,404)	1071
mome filter 1 -None	(50,481)	(79,404)	1072

Figure 51- Momentum Filter 4 Combinations Perform The Best

But they have a low number of trades, so they are considered suspect. So, that leaves us with this:

BEST NET PROFIT			
Filter	profit	drawdown	trades
mome filter 3	(5,589)	(35,068)	93
mome filter 2	(7,152)	(38,054)	139
mome bbf filter 2	(7,461)	(37,289)	155
mome bbf filter 3	(10,236)	(27,321)	259
mome bbf filter 1 -None	(50,480)	(79,404)	1071
mome filter 1 -None	(50,481)	(79,404)	1072

BEST DRAWDOWN			
Filter	profit	drawdown	trades
mome bbf filter 3	(10,236)	(27,321)	259
mome filter 3	(5,589)	(35,068)	93
mome bbf filter 2	(7,461)	(37,289)	155
mome filter 2	(7,152)	(38,054)	139
mome bbf filter 1 -None	(50,480)	(79,404)	1071
mome filter 1 -None	(50,481)	(79,404)	1072

Figure 52 - Filter 3 Combinations Are Superior

This data is not conclusive, since the best profit filter is not the lowest drawdown filter. If you desire the best net profit, then "mome filter #3" (double momentum filter) is best, and if low drawdown is the goal, then that same filter with closing all trades during flat periods is probably best.

Big Takeaways From Study, To This Point
1. Bull/Bear/Flat Filters Work Better Than Having No Filters

2. With Such Varying Results Across Filters, It Is Good To Verify Filters For Your Particular Strategy

The best way to incorporate what I've done is to take my ideas, add them to your strategies and test them out. See what works and doesn't work. This study isn't meant to be "use XXXX as a filter" or anything definitive like that. Rather, it is to give you ideas and concepts for you to incorporate into your own algo trading. That is where the real benefit is.

Now we will take a short detour, and instead of filtering for bull/bear, we will filter for volatile and non-volatile periods. For volume and volatility, there are a few schools of thought.

With volume, some traders think that larger than normal volume means something significant is happening in the market. Lots of people are trading, the thinking goes, and therefore some significant price movement is in store. A great time to trade!

Of course, there is an opposite view. Lower than average volume could signal indecision and uncertainty. This could happen before an explosive move. So, maybe the best time to trade is with low volume?

I don't know the answer, although I will say that based on my experience, the "trade with low volume setups" tends to work better. But maybe that is just my testing, I don't know. So, I'll test both high and low volume approaches.

A similar conundrum exists for volatility, which I'll measure with the Average True Range. Maybe if the current Average True Range is higher than normal, it is a good time to trade. Conversely, maybe a lower than normal Average True range is a better time. I honestly don't know which is preferable, so I'll test both.

I am going to test 9 different filters (I'll refer to them as "VolVol" filters, for Volatility and Volume):

VolVol Filter #1
Always allow trades (no filter baseline)

VolVol Filter #2
Allow trades only if 1 bar ATR (Average True Range) is ABOVE average ATR over the last 100,150 or 200 bars

VolVol Filter #3
Allow trades only if 1 bar ATR (Average True Range) is BELOW average ATR over the last 100,150 or 200 bars

VolVol Filter #4

Allow trades only if current bar volume is ABOVE average volume over the last 100,150 or 200 bars

VolVol Filter #5

Allow trades only if current bar volume is BELOW average volume over the last 100,150 or 200 bars

Filters 6-9 are combination filters for both volume and volatility:

VolVol Filter #6

Allow trades only if 1 bar ATR (Average True Range) is ABOVE average ATR over the last 100,150 or 200 bars AND if current bar volume is ABOVE average volume over the last 100,150 or 200 bars

VolVol Filter #7

Allow trades only if 1 bar ATR (Average True Range) is ABOVE average ATR over the last 100,150 or 200 bars AND if current bar volume is BELOW average volume over the last 100,150 or 200 bars

VolVol Filter #8

Allow trades only if 1 bar ATR (Average True Range) is BELOW average ATR over the last 100,150 or 200 bars AND if current bar volume is ABOVE average volume over the last 100,150 or 200 bars

VolVol Filter #9

Allow trades only if 1 bar ATR (Average True Range) is BELOW average ATR over the last 100,150 or 200 bars AND if current bar volume is BELOW average volume over the last 100,150 or 200 bars

All together, we are running 129,600 unique cases.

Results

Row Labels	Average of Net Profit	Average of Max Intraday Drawdown
volvol filter 1 -None	($50,477.7)	($79,402.1)
volvol filter 2	($75,397.0)	($83,301.9)
volvol filter 3	($67,797.2)	($74,895.8)
volvol filter 4	($57,377.0)	($65,139.8)
volvol filter 5	($64,769.3)	($73,125.3)
volvol filter 6	($53,086.5)	($59,474.7)
volvol filter 7	($20,329.0)	($23,169.7)
volvol filter 8	($34,324.8)	($38,816.8)
volvol filter 9	($62,053.9)	($67,784.5)
Grand Total	($53,956.9)	($62,790.1)

Figure 53- Volatility And Volume Filter Results (Green/Gray = Better)

The results are somewhat underwhelming for most of the filters.

For filters 2 and 3, the average true range filters, Net Profit is worse, and the Max Drawdown is not much changed.

For filters 4 and 5, the volume filters, Net Profit is worse, but the Max Drawdown is somewhat less.

For all 4 of those, there is not enough evidence to say "we've found the Holy Grail!" :(:(

For the combination filters 6-9, filters 7 & 8 both have improved Net Profit and reduced Maximum Drawdown. These cases also have a lot less trades when compared to the baseline case. This suggests that the filters are doing their job, and reducing the number of bad trades.

Row Labels	Average of Total Trades
volvol filter 1 -None	1071.4
volvol filter 2	1590.7
volvol filter 3	1428.4
volvol filter 4	1206.9
volvol filter 5	1350.2
volvol filter 6	1124.7
volvol filter 7	428.6
volvol filter 8	711.5
volvol filter 9	1301.9
Grand Total	1134.9

Figure 54- Volatility And Volume Filters, Impact On Number Of Trades

What is interesting about filters 7 and 8 is that they are exact opposites, and both do well. Filter 7 likes above average volatility, and lower than normal volume. Filter 8 likes below average volatility, and higher than normal volume.

Here are sample results, with filter #7 and filter #8:

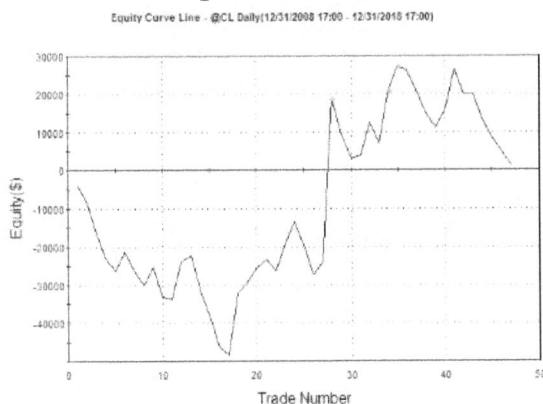

Crude Oil, Strategy #1, With No VolVol Filter

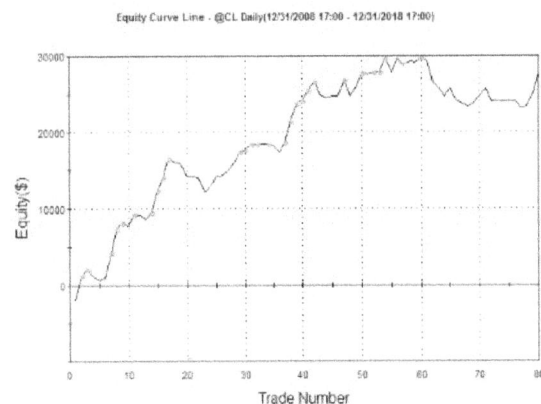

Crude Oil, Strategy #1, With VolVol Filter #7 (note MORE trades)

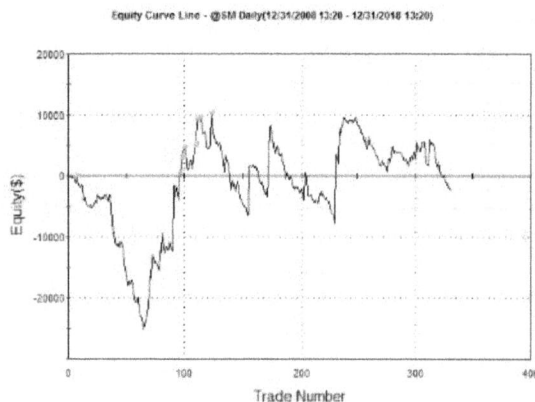

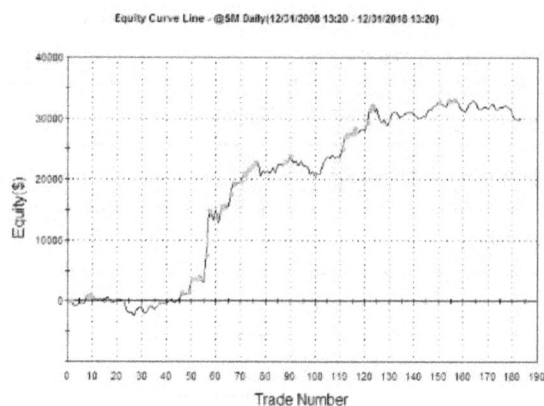

Soybean Meal, Strategy #5,
No VolVol Filter

Soybean Meal, Strategy #5, With
VolVol Filter #8

Figure 55- Sample Results With VolVol Filters

Of course, there are cases where the filters make things worse, but based on the overall numbers, MOST times using filters #7 or #8 should improve performance.

What I'd Be Testing, Based Volatility and Volume Tests

I would test strategies with the following filters:

VolVol Filter #7

Allow trades only if 1 bar ATR (Average True Range) is ABOVE average ATR over the last 100,150 or 200 bars AND if current bar volume is BELOW average volume over the last 100,150 or 200 bars.

VolVol Filter #8

Allow trades only if 1 bar ATR (Average True Range) is BELOW average ATR over the last 100,150 or 200 bars AND if current bar volume is ABOVE average volume over the last 100,150 or 200 bars.

If you do not want to optimize for the long period length, I recommend 150 bars, as that is right in the middle of the range. Then you can save your optimization for other variables!

Putting It All Together

As a final evaluation, I'll test the following side by side:

Filter # 1 - No filter

Filter #2 – Part 2 - Simple Momentum Bull/Bear Filter

Filter #3 – Part 2 - Simple Momentum Bull/Bear Filter, with VolVol filter #7

Filter #4 – Part 2 - Simple Momentum Bull/Bear Filter, with VolVol filter #8

Filter #5 – Last Section of Part 2 - Simple Momentum Bull/Bear/Flat Filter

Filter #6 – Last Section of Part 2 - Simple Momentum Bull/Bear/Flat Filter, with VolVol filter #7

Filter #7 – Last Section of Part 2 - Simple Momentum Bull/Bear/Flat Filter, with VolVol filter #8

These case were generally the best ones from the previous sections.

Results

Row Labels	Average of Net Profit	Average of Max Intraday Drawdown
filter 1 -None	($50,477.7)	($79,402.1)
filter 2	($7,455.9)	($37,286.0)
filter 3	($18,450.2)	($21,570.6)
filter 4	($9,420.9)	($11,867.7)
filter 5	($10,235.0)	($27,321.7)
filter 6	($14,341.4)	($17,031.7)
filter 7	($7,082.0)	($9,132.0)
Grand Total	($16,780.5)	($29,087.4)

Figure 56- Final Composite Results

When viewed over all 40 instruments, 5 bar sizes and 8 different strategies, overall the data shows:

Bull/Bear/Flat filter is better than plain Bull/Bear filter (for drawdown, not profit – compare filters #2 and #5)

VolVol filter #8 is better than VolVol #7, when combined with Bull/Bear Filter

Filter #7 (Bull/Bear/Flat filter with Volvol #8 filter is best overall)

This filter reduces the number of trades by quite a bit, and consequently filters out a lot of bad trades (a very good thing!)

Row Labels	Average of Total Trades
filter 1 -None	1071.4
filter 2	154.8
filter 3	356.2
filter 4	214.6
filter 5	259.2
filter 6	271.6
filter 7	164.4
Grand Total	356.0

Figure 57- Filter #7 Reduces Number Of Trades Significantly

But, a legitimate question to ask at this point is: "Sure, Net Profit improves, and Max Drawdown is lower, but how do you know that this is not just due to filtering? In other words, maybe the filters are just getting rid of a lot of trades – good and bad – and not necessarily just the bad ones!"

That is the problem with big datasets and lots of performance numbers. You can easily draw different conclusions based on which data you look at. So, let's look at a few different numbers, one familiar, one not so familiar.

Average Net Profit Per Trade is a great way to see if the filters are filtering out primarily bad trades, or if they are just filtering out all trades:

Row Labels ⌄	Average of Total Trades	Avg New Trade	Improvement
filter 1 -None	1071.4	($47.12)	
filter 2	154.8	($48.16)	-2.2%
filter 3	356.2	($51.80)	-10.0%
filter 4	214.6	($43.89)	6.8%
filter 5	259.2	($39.49)	16.2%
filter 6	271.6	($52.81)	-12.1%
filter 7	164.4	($43.09)	8.5%
Grand Total	356.0		

Figure 58- Average Profit Per Trade Results

This shows that Filters #5 and #7 are the best. Filter #5 is the simple momentum Bull/Bear/Flat filter, and Filter #7 is just Filter #5 the volume and volatility filter added on. So, using Average Trade suggests that Filter #5 is actually best.

Another way to look at the data is to step back and look at the big picture. What are we really trying to do here with these filters? Really, we are trying to eliminate bad outcomes, while still keeping the good outcomes.

One way to see this is by categorizing results for each iteration relative to Net Profit. For example, having an iteration with overall Net Profit above $25,000 for the test duration could be considered a "good" outcome. Conversely, a Net Profit less than -$25,000 (a big loser!) could be considered a bad outcome.

So, let's take a look at this uncommon metric:

When you look at the number of cases with more than $25K Net Profit, Filter #2 is the clear winner, and when you look at removing bad cases, Filter #7 is the best:

Row Labels	Sum of >$25000 Net Profit
filter 1 -None	1,413
filter 2	2,076
filter 3	5
filter 4	27
filter 5	906
filter 6	4
filter 7	22
Grand Total	4,453

Row Labels	Sum of <-$25000 Net Profit
filter 1 -None	6,858
filter 2	3,866
filter 3	3,023
filter 4	1,623
filter 5	3,344
filter 6	2,337
filter 7	1,133
Grand Total	22,184

Figure 59- Impact of Filters On "Good" And "Bad" Results

But both measures have drawbacks. For example, while filter #7 removes a lot of bad outcomes, it also removes a lot of good outcomes – only 22 "very profitable" cases remain!

So maybe a ratio metric is in order - the ratio of very profitable cases to very unprofitable cases:

Filter Type	Ratio of Good/Bad
filter 1 -None	0.21
filter 2	0.54
filter 3	0.00
filter 4	0.02
filter 5	0.27
filter 6	0.00
filter 7	0.02

Figure 60 - Ratio Of Good/Bad Results

The best one is now filter #2, since it has so many good outcomes relative to bad outcomes.

This tells us then that the filter to choose really depends on what is most important to you:

Maximizing Net Profit
Minimizing Max Drawdown
Maximizing Average Profit Per Trade
Maximizing Good Results / Bad Results

What is best for me might not be best for you!

In any event, here is a sample of the progress we've made in this chapter.

First, we start out with a simple strategy (strategy #5 for this example). It does not look too great…

CanTradeLong=True; //no filter
CanTradeShort=True; //no filter
if CanTradeLong = True and close> close [inputvar2] then buy next bar at market;
if CanTradeShort = True and close <close [inputvar2] then sellshort next bar at market;

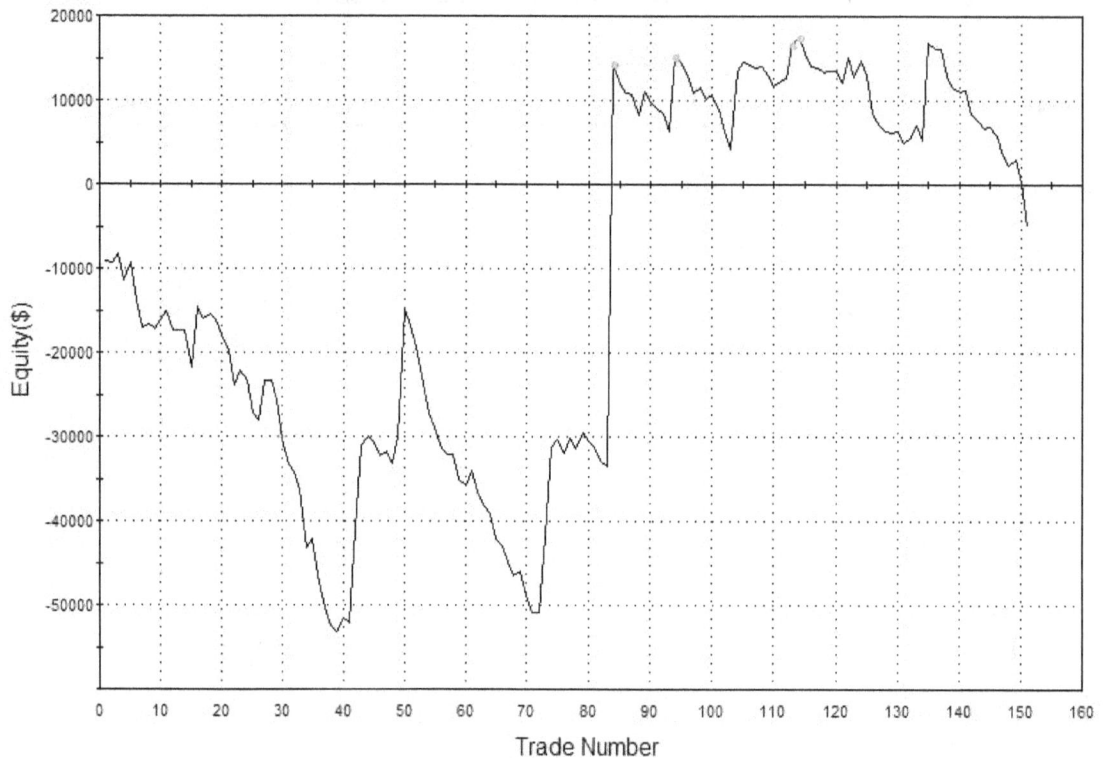

Figure 61- Original Strategy Results

Then, we added a bull/bear momentum filter to it.

> *CanTradeLong = False;*
> *CanTradeShort = False;*
> *If close> close [InputVar4] Then CanTradeLong = True;*
> *If close <close [InputVar4] Then CanTradeShort = True;*
> *if CanTradeLong = True and close> close [inputvar2] then buy next bar at market;*
>
> *if CanTradeShort = True and close <close [inputvar2] then sellshort next bar at market;*

Yikes! Looks like we are headed the wrong way…

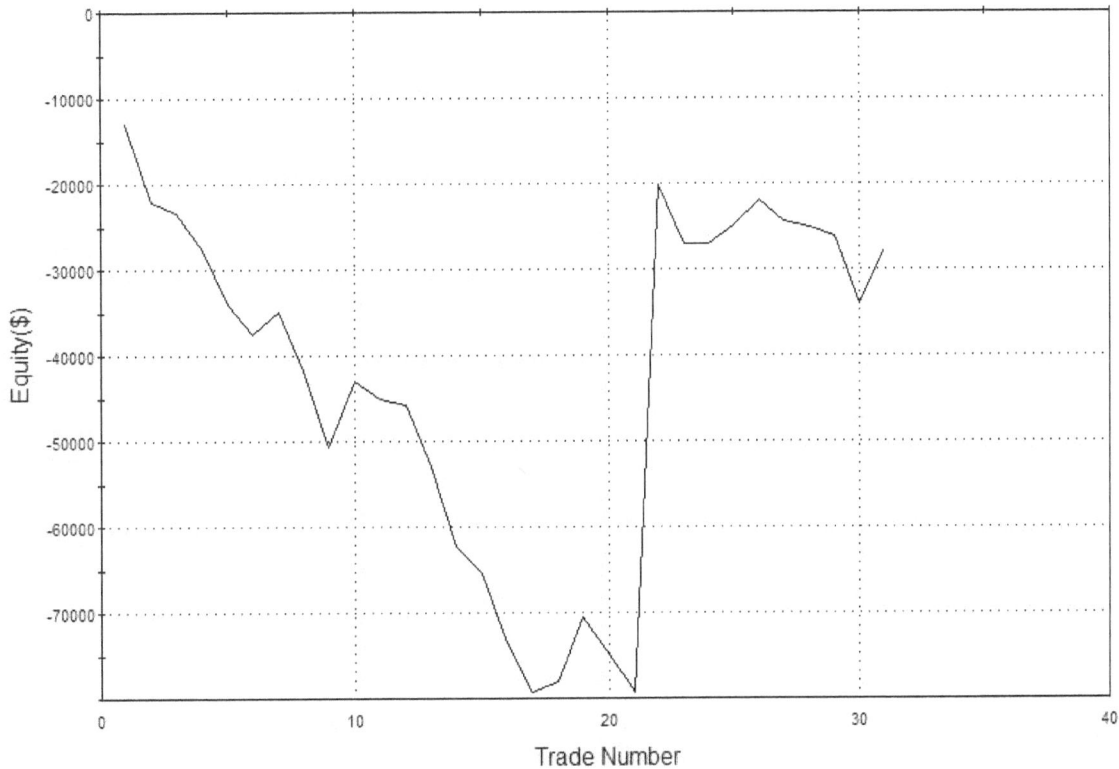

Figure 62 - Simple Momentum Filter Was Not An Improvement

Note in the chart above that there are only 31 trades in the 10 year period. Watch out for that - a small number of trades - when doing any testing. The smaller the number of trades, the less reliable the results will be.

Next, we added a volume and volatility filter to the scheme.

// momentum with volvol filter 8

CanTradeLong = False;

CanTradeShort = False;

If close> close [InputVar4] and Volume>averagefc(volume,InputVar4) and AvgTrueRange(1)<AvgTrueRange(InputVar4) Then CanTradeLong = True;

If close <close [InputVar4] and Volume>averagefc(volume,InputVar4) and AvgTrueRange(1)<AvgTrueRange(InputVar4)Then CanTradeShort = True;

if CanTradeLong = True and close> close [inputvar2] then buy next bar at market;

if CanTradeShort = True and close <close [inputvar2] then sellshort next bar at market;

Now things are looking better!

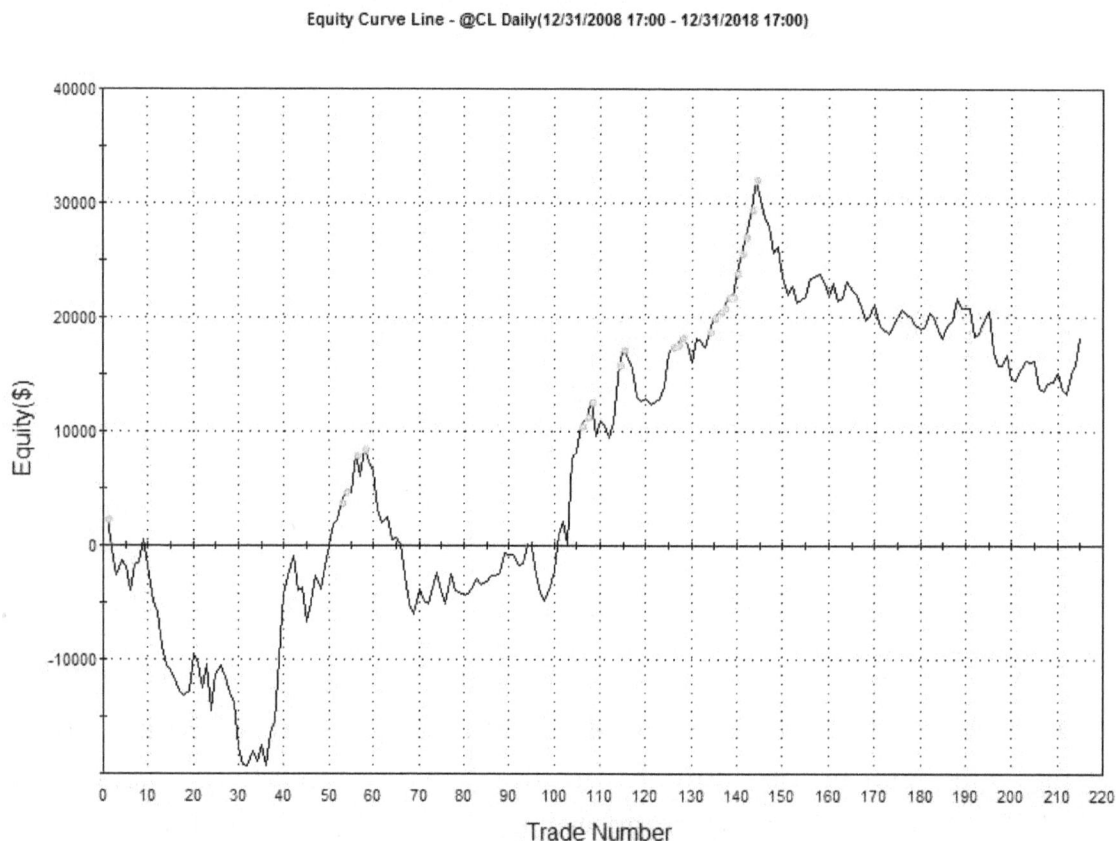

Equity Curve Line - @CL Daily(12/31/2008 17:00 - 12/31/2018 17:00)

Figure 63 - Improved Performance With Volume And Volatility Filter

Finally, we change the bull/bear filter into a bull/bear/flat filter. From the original strategy, we have improved the Net Profit by $34,730, and reduced the Max Drawdown by $32,595.

// momentum with flat period and volvol filter 8
CanTradeLong = False;
CanTradeShort = False;
If close> close [InputVar4] and close> close [InputVar4/2] and

Volume>averagefc(volume,InputVar4)   and   AvgTrueRange(1) <AvgTrueRange(InputVar4) Then CanTradeLong = True;

If close <close [InputVar4] and close <close [InputVar4/2] and Volume>averagefc(volume,InputVar4)   and   AvgTrueRange(1) <AvgTrueRange(InputVar4) Then CanTradeShort = True;

if CanTradeLong = True and close> close [inputvar2] then buy next bar at market;

if CanTradeShort = True and close <close [inputvar2] then sellshort next bar at market;

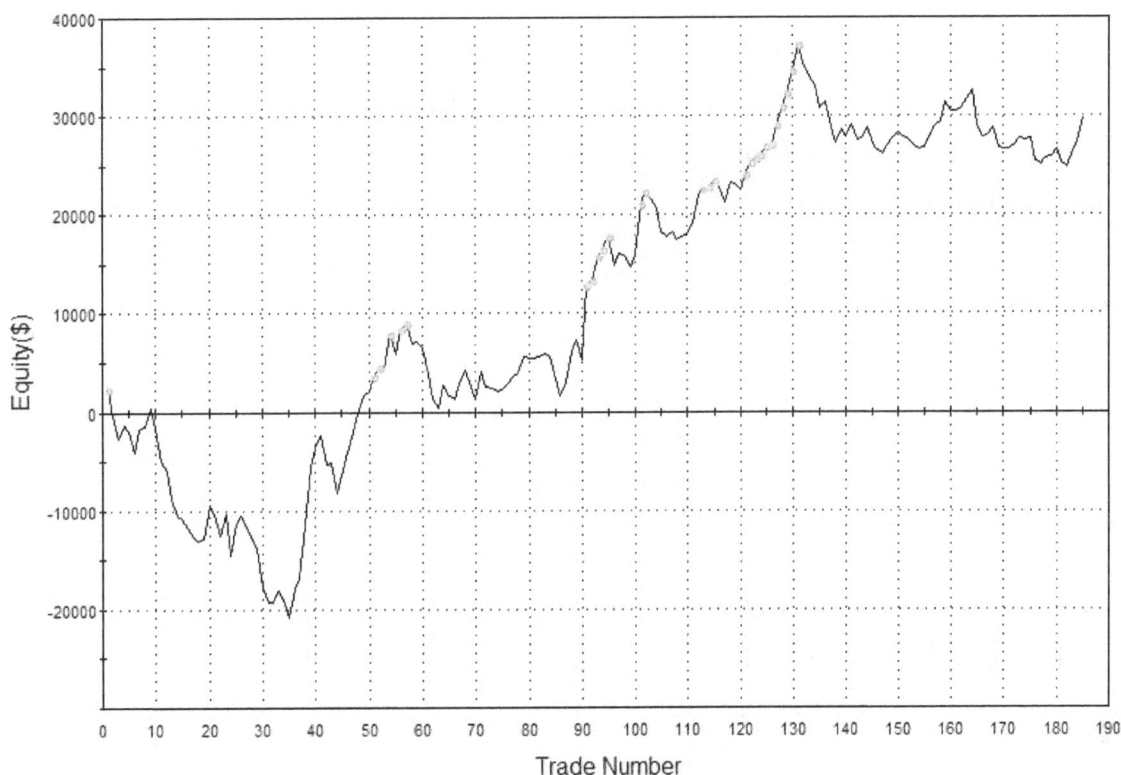

Equity Curve Line - @CL Daily(12/31/2008 17:00 - 12/31/2018 17:00)

Figure 64 - Addition Of Flat Filter

The best part of this transformation is that it is not just for specific cases. This improvement seems to hold up over many strategies, markets and timeframes.

Now realize this is just an example – you MUST test your particular situation. Maybe this filtering will help your strategy, but there is a chance it will not help.

Algo Trading Cheat Codes

*What I'd Be Testing, Based On This Study – Option 1

// momentum with flat period and volvol filter 8

CanTradeLong = False;

CanTradeShort = False;

//Set InputVar4 to between 100 and 200 (not much difference from 100 to 200)

If close> close [InputVar4] and close> close [InputVar4/2] and Volume>averagefc(volume,InputVar4) and AvgTrueRange(1) <AvgTrueRange(InputVar4) Then CanTradeLong = True;

If close <close [InputVar4] and close <close [InputVar4/2] and Volume>averagefc(volume,InputVar4) and AvgTrueRange(1) <AvgTrueRange(InputVar4) Then CanTradeShort = True;

if CanTradeLong = True and YOUR LONG ENTRY then buy next bar at market;

if CanTradeShort = True and YOUR SHORT ENTRY then sellshort next bar at market;

* What I'd Be Testing, Based On This Study – Option 2

// momentum buy/bear filter only

CanTradeLong = False;

CanTradeShort = False;

//Set InputVar4 to between 100 and 200 (not much difference from 100 to 200)

If close> close [InputVar4] Then CanTradeLong = True;

If close <close [InputVar4] Then CanTradeShort = True;

if CanTradeLong = True and YOUR LONG ENTRY then buy next bar at market;

if CanTradeShort = True and YOUR SHORT ENTRY then sellshort next bar at market;

* Trend Based Bull/Bear/Flat Regime filters on average improve net

profit, and reduce drawdown

    * Volume and Volatility based filters can improve results

    * As with all filters, it is advised to add the filters to your strategy BEFORE you do full testing

CHAPTER 8 – EXIT TESTING

Ask any trader how they trade, and 8 times out of 10 the answer will involve the entries they use to trade:

"When the trendline is confirmed, I enter."

"When the close is above the 9 bar moving average and the RSI is not oversold, I go long."

"When the order flow suggests a downwards push, I go short."

If you need any more proof of the popularity of entries, just look at trading videos on YouTube. Most of them are focused on entries. Even my You Tube channel, which hits on a variety of trading topics, has entry videos as its most popular selections.

But entries are only part of the story. Money management, psychology and position sizing all play a role. And, of course, exits. Many times exits are even more important than entries!

So, to give exits their long deserved recognition, I am going to study a variety of them, with some fairly standard entries. Which exit is the best? That is what I hope to determine in this chapter.

What Exits Should I Choose?

If you have read this far in this book, you know I favor simplicity over complexity. My experience is simple strategies tend to hold up better over time than complicated, multi-variable strategies. Therefore, to get a wide range of exits, I am going to examine some "simple" exits, some "intermediate" level exits and some "complicated" exits:

Simple Exits
1. Stop and Reverse Exit
2. Time Based Exit
3. Dollar Stop Loss
4. Dollar Profit Target
5. Dollar Stop With Profit Target
6. Average True Range Stop Loss
7. Average True Range Profit Target
8. Average True Range Stop With Profit Target

Intermediate Complexity Exits
9. Trailing Stop
10 Breakeven Stop

Complicated Exits
11. Parabolic Stop
12. Chandelier Stop
13. Yo-Yo Stop
14. Channel Exit
15. Moving Average Exit

Each of these exits will be described in a later section. For each exit, I will run 9 different combinations of the exit parameter or parameters.

I should point out I do NOT use market on close MOC orders in this study. Why not? At least with Tradestation, these orders do not work in real trading, except in specific circumstances.

Entries, Markets, And Everything Else

I'll test each of the 15 exits with 5 unique entries (Tradestation code shown):

1. Simple Momentum Entry

If close>close[InputVar2] then buy next bar at market;
If close<close[InputVar2] then sell short next bar at market;

2. Breakout Next Bar Entry

If high=highest(high,InputVar2) then buy next bar at market;
If low=lowest(low,InputVar2) then sell short next bar at market;

3. Single Moving Average Cross Entry

If close crosses above average(close,InputVar2) then buy next bar at market;
If close crosses below average(close,InputVar2) then sell short next bar at market;

4. Bollinger Band Entry

If close crosses above BollingerBand(close, InputVar2, -2) then buy next bar at market;
If close crosses below BollingerBand(close, InputVar2, +2) then sell short next bar at market;

5. Volatility Entry

*If Close> close[1] + AvgTrueRange(InputVar2) * 1.5 then buy next bar at market;*
*If Close< close[1] - AvgTrueRange(InputVar2) * 1.5 then sellshort next bar at market;*

Note that there is one input to optimize for the entry, the input "InputVar2." This is a lookback length, and for the study I will vary this from 15 to 35 in steps of 10.

Markets

I am going to test the exits on 40 different futures markets (Tradestation continuous contract symbols shown).

Currencies

@AD, @BP, @CD, @DX, @EC, @JY, @SF

Ags/Softs

@BO, @C, @CC, @CT, @FC, @KC, @KW, @LC, @LH, @O, @OJ, @RR, @S, @SB, @SM, @W

Metals

@GC, @HG, @PL, @SI

Energies

@CL, @HO, @NG, @RB

Interest Rates

@FV, @TY, @US

Stock Indices

@ES.D (day session),@ES, @NK, @NQ, @RTY, @YM

Bar Sizes

Since results can vary dramatically depending on the size of the bar that is tested, I will test 5 different bar sizes:

60 minute
120 minute
360 minute
720 minute
1440 minute (daily)

Test Period

I will run all cases thru 10 years of historical data, from Jan 1, 2010 to Jan 1, 2020.

Other Test Criteria

As always, I will include proper amounts for slippage and commission in the study. Each market has its own value for slippage, based upon its liquidity and volume. I'll use values that I have determined from real money trading, and also from in-depth analysis of market quotes and prices.

For some of the exits, the use of "Look Inside Bar Backtesting - LIBB" is necessary to get accurate results. If you do not know what LIBB is, or why it is important, check out this video, starting at 8:02: https://youtu.be/tNWdJeHRZNE?t=482

How To Compare Results

Of course, when comparing 567,000 tests, the question "how do you determine what is best?" will inevitably come up.

I am going to look at 2 different metrics:

Return on Account = Total Net Profit / Maximum Drawdown (shown in charts and tables as "Average of Return On Account")

# of Cases With Net Profit > $25K = High Net Profit Cases (shown in charts and tables as "Sum of Prof > $25K")

Of course, I could write a whole chapter on why I chose these particular metrics, and someone could counter with reasons why other performance metrics would be better.

My goal here was to compare risk adjusted returns, and also to identify which combinations produced a "good" overall Net Profit. My personal experience is that when both of these metrics are mediocre, chances are the strategy entry and exit just are not that good.

Summary Of Testing

40 markets x 5 Bar Sizes x 5 Entries x 3 Lengths per Entry x 15 Exits x 9 Settings Per Exit = 405,000 Unique Tests (later on I will add in more exits to the study, which will increase the test total to 567,000)

If you work with Tradestation at all, you'll soon realize that all of this testing would be very tedious and time consuming! To speed up testing, I'll use Multi-Opt, specialized software which uses Tradestation's OOEL (Object Oriented Easy Language) and the Tradestation Optimization API. The Tradestation API is free to all Tradestation users, so you could create your own "speed testing" tool with some time and effort.

With my testing setup, running all the cases actually took over 100 hours of non-stop testing, even after utilizing multi-threading.

IMPORTANT NOTE:

I'll be showing the results I obtained from this testing; if you run tests yourself, you may get different results, and therefore reach different conclusions. You may program entries and exits differently than I did, or you may use different ranges for variables than I did.

And just because Exit A is better overall than Exit B with average performance metrics, it does not mean it is always better. Maybe certain markets or bar sizes work better with Exit B than Exit A, for example.

The point here is that you can use the results I found to guide your research in testing, but ALWAYS verify results with your own testing/analysis. At the end of the day, you are going to be the person trading your account, so you should also be the person testing your particular strategies.

That being said, this study can be a huge time saver for you. For instance, why bother testing systems with the worst exit? Focus on the good results first!

Baseline (Stop and Reverse) Exit Results, and Time Based Exit Results

Stop and Reverse

If close>close[InputVar2] then buy next bar at market;
If close<close[InputVar2] then sell short next bar at market;

It might seem like the Tradestation Easy Language code has no exit at all, but that is not the case. With Tradestation, a "buy" comment means 2 things. First, any short is exited. Second, a long position is initiated. Vice versa for short trades. Thus, these standard buy/sell short keywords are stop and reverse commands.

For the stop and reverse exit case, that is the only exit – a reverse in position. These strategies are then, by definition, always in the market.

I should point out for this study that all exit cases include stop and reverse built in. That is because of the code show above. As mentioned previously, this code will reverse an existing position. And that is what I used for all the cases I am running.

As an alternative (I'll leave the reader to test this), I could have run entry code like this:

If mp=0 and close>close[InputVar2] then buy next bar at market;
If mp=0 close<close[InputVar2] then sell short next bar at market;

"mp" refers to market position, so with the code above, the entries are only activated if the current position is flat (mp=0). There is no stop and reverse for this code.

If you try such code, just remember to have other exits in the strategy; otherwise the strategy may enter a position and never exit!

Time Based Exit

If the trader assumes an entry signal will be "good" only for a certain number of bars, exiting after a certain number of bars makes a lot of sense. It has been said that legendary trader John Henry favors this type of exit.

In Tradestation, the code looks like this:

If MP=1 and BarsSinceEntry>InputVar4*5 then sell next bar market; //exit long trades

If MP=-1 and BarsSinceEntry>InputVar4*5 then buytocover next bar market; //exit short trades

I've set up InputVar4 to vary from 1 to 9, so with this exit, the strategy will stay in the trade for 5 to 45 bars after entry.

Now on to the results…with all the data, the results are pretty clear: Stop and Reverse Exits are much better than Time Based Exits.

Row Labels	Average of Return on Account
Stop & Reverse Exit	-7.9
Time Based Exit	-25.9
Grand Total	-16.9

Row Labels	Sum of Prof>$25K
Stop & Reverse Exit	3528
Time Based Exit	2355
Grand Total	5883

Figure 65 - Stop & Reverse Vs. Time Based Exits

Stop & Reverse Exits provide a higher Average Return on Account, and produce more "highly profitable" cases (after adjusting for the fact that Stop and Reverse exits have only one exit value, while time based exits have 9 values).

The other interesting thing to note is that overall, both exits lose money over the 10 year test, on average. Of course, a lot of that could be due to the markets chosen, the entries and the bar sizes.

Let's see what breaking down the data a bit further looks like…

By Market Sector

When viewed by market sector, Stop & Reverse is always better than the Time Based Exit. And the only sectors, on average, that make money are Metals and the Stock Indices. This could be because of the trendiness of those sectors, as compared to other sectors.

Average of Return on Account	Colun ▾							
Row Labels ▾	Ags	Curr	Energ	Metals	Rates	Softs	Stock	Grand Total
Stop & Reverse Exit	-25.9	-19.2	-20.0	9.7	-26.6	-32.0	64.2	-7.9
Time Based Exit	-34.8	-34.4	-33.4	-1.3	-54.3	-37.2	12.1	-25.9
Grand Total	-30.3	-26.8	-26.7	4.2	-40.4	-34.6	38.2	-16.9

Sum of Prof>$25K	Column Labels ▾							
Row Labels ▾	Ags	Curr	Energ	Metals	Rates	Softs	Stock	Grand Total
Stop & Reverse Exit	396	432	414	693	99	216	1278	3528
Time Based Exit	301	221	307	555	36	146	789	2355
Grand Total	697	653	721	1248	135	362	2067	5883

Figure 66- Results By Market Sector

By Bar Size

As shown in a previous chapter, large bar sizes tend to be better for trading systems. Whether this is due to reduced noise in the larger bar sizes, or possibly getting further from the realm of high frequency trading firms, all other things being equal, daily bars are more profitable than 60 minute bars.

As shown in the tables below, the worst results are with the shortest bar – the 60 minute bars. The best bars are actually 720 minute (12 hours), followed by 1440 minute bars.

Average of Return on Account	Colun ▾					
Row Labels	▾ 120min	360min	60min	720min	1440min	Grand Total
Stop & Reverse Exit	-29.9	3.5	-58.9	26.4	19.4	-7.9
Time Based Exit	-53.7	-15.7	-78.5	7.2	10.9	-25.9
Grand Total	**-41.8**	**-6.1**	**-68.7**	**16.8**	**15.2**	**-16.9**

Sum of Prof>$25K	Column Labels ▾					
Row Labels	▾ 120min	360min	60min	720min	1440min	Grand Total
Stop & Reverse Exit	513	846	252	1008	909	3528
Time Based Exit	204	549	49	795	758	2355
Grand Total	**717**	**1395**	**301**	**1803**	**1667**	**5883**

Figure 67 - Results For Different Bar Sizes

By Entry Type

I've previously done separate studies on entries before, and the conclusion was that breakout entries were superior to other common entries.

Results for this study confirm those earlier results.

Best entries for Stop & Reverse Exit:
1. Breakout
2. Bollinger Bands
3. Volatility Break
4. Momentum

5. Moving Average Cross

Best entries for Time Based Exit:
1. Bollinger Bands
2. Volatility Break
3. Breakout
4. Moving Average Cross
5. Momentum

For both exits, the top 3 entries were Bollinger Bands, Volatility Break and Breakout. And for 4 of the 5 entries, the Stop & Reverse exit was better than the time based exit.

Average of Return on Account	Column Labels					
Row Labels	Bollinger Band	Breakout	Momentum	Mov Avg Cross	Volatility Break	Grand Total
Stop & Reverse Exit	25.3	27.2	-46.4	-52.5	7.1	-7.9
Time Based Exit	-2.4	-15.6	-54.2	-50.5	-7.2	-25.9
Grand Total	11.5	5.8	-50.3	-51.5	-0.1	-16.9

Sum of Prof>$25K	Column Labels					
Row Labels	Bollinger Band	Breakout	Momentum	Mov Avg Cross	Volatility Break	Grand Total
Stop & Reverse Exit	1080	981	351	261	855	3528
Time Based Exit	667	622	295	289	482	2355
Grand Total	1747	1603	646	550	1337	5883

Figure 68- Results For Different Entries

Conclusion – Stop & Reverse Vs. Time Based Exits

From this study, it is pretty clear that the Stop & Reverse is a better exit than the Time Based Exit, regardless of the market sector, bar size or practically any other parameter.

Of course, that does not mean time based exits should be discarded, but it is good to know that many times they might just add system complexity without adding any real value.

Algo Trading Cheat Code:

* When Developing a Strategy, First Try Stop & Reverse Exits, Before Adding in Time Based Exits

Part 2 – Other Simple Exits

In this section I'll look at 6 relatively simple exits – can any of these outperform the stop and reverse exit?

First I'll start with dollar based stops and targets. In another study I did, I showed in some situations ATR stops were better than dollar stops. But, this is a different study, and we will see if we reach different conclusions.

For all testing, the input "InputVar4" runs from 1 to 9. So, the stop values in dollars per contract will run from $500 to $4500. Profit targets will run from $1000 to $9000. Finally for the value of InputVar=9, there is no stop loss or profit target.

Dollar Stop

Pretty much as simple as it gets. Having just this exit will let profits run until the reverse entry takes you out. No limit on potential profit.

SetStopLoss(InputVar4*500); //Dollar Stop Exit

Dollar Target

This profit target uses a limit order, so you should check to make sure that your platform will fill limit orders only if the limit price is exceeded.

This exit alone can be dangerous, as you are looking for the reverse entry to exit any bad trades. The loss on a trade could be significant. On the flipside, you are limiting your profit by having a target, which may not turn out to be a good idea.

SetProfitTarget(InputVar4*1000); //Dollar Target Exit

Dollar Stop Loss and Dollar Target Together

This exit has both a stop loss and a profit target. I have arbitrarily picked the profit level to be 2x the stop level. This obviously could be something that is optimized, but I chose not to for this study.

*SetStopLoss(InputVar4*500); //Dollar Stop Exit*

*SetProfitTarget(InputVar4*1000); //Dollar Target Exit (2 times stop level)*

Average True Range Exits

ATR Stop
ATR based exits are calculated using the 14 bar Average True Range. No limit on potential profit.

*SetStopLoss(BigPointValue*InputVar4*AvgTrueRange(14)/3);*

ATR Target
This profit target uses a limit order based on average true range. It has many of the same issues as the dollar target.

*SetProfitTarget(BigPointValue*InputVar4*AvgTrueRange(14)/1.5);*

ATR Stop Loss and Dollar Target
This exit has both a stop loss and a profit target. I have arbitrarily picked the profit level to be 2x the stop level - maybe I'll do a study optimizing that value in the future…

*SetStopLoss(BigPointValue*InputVar4*AvgTrueRange(14)/3);*

*SetProfitTarget(BigPointValue*InputVar4*AvgTrueRange(14)/1.5);*

Overall Results

Row Labels	Average of Return on Account
Stop & Reverse Exit	-7.9
Dollar Target Exit	-10.5
Dollar Stop Exit	-19.2
ATR Target Exit	-21.2
Dollar Stop/Target Exit	-22.6
Time Based Exit	-25.9
ATR Stop Exit	-27.0
ATR Stop/Target Exit	-42.8
Grand Total	-22.1

Row Labels	Sum of Prof>$25K
Stop & Reverse Exit	3528
Dollar Target Exit	3238
ATR Target Exit	2696
Dollar Stop Exit	2691
ATR Stop Exit	2383
Time Based Exit	2355
Dollar Stop/Target Exit	2310
ATR Stop/Target Exit	1626
Grand Total	20827

Figure 69 - Results For Simple Exits

Results can be summarized as follows:

* Stop & Reverse Exit is still the best.
* Dollar based exits are generally better than ATR exits.
Target exits are generally better than stop exits.
* Of all 3 combinations (stop, target or stop/target), the stop/target is always the worst.

The findings here are generally in line with the results of an earlier study I did. In that study, I found stop and reverse ("no exit" in earlier study) was the best, and ATR was a bit better than dollar exits (this study shows dollar exits are a bit better). This could be because of different strategies used, different performance metrics, etc.

I think the major takeaway is that the Stop & Reverse Exit still reigns supreme!

Figure 70 - Best And Worst Exit Types

By Market Sector, Bar Size and Entry Type

For just about every market sector, Stop & Reverse is the winner. 2nd best is the Dollar Target exit. This flies in the face of the common market adage "let your profits run." Maybe you only let your profits run up to a point. Interesting!

Bar size analysis leads you to Stop & Reverse with 1440 minute bars as being the best.

Maybe some entries work best with certain exits. What does the data tell us? Once again, for the most part, Stop & Reverse exits are the best.

Summary tables for market sector, Bar Size and Entry Type are shown below.

Average of Return on Account   Column Labels ▾

Row Labels ↓T	Ags	Curr	Energ	Metals	Rates	Softs	Stock	Grand Total
Stop & Reverse Exit	-25.9	-19.2	-20.0	9.7	-26.6	-32.05	64.2	-7.9
Dollar Target Exit	-27.2	-15.6	-24.5	-1.3	-26.8	-32.00	55.3	-10.5
ATR Target Exit	-41.0	-19.2	-32.4	-7.3	-37.3	-41.7	36.2	-21.2
Dollar Stop Exit	-29.1	-27.4	-29.7	-12.9	-35.6	-36.8	34.1	-19.2
ATR Stop Exit	-39.1	-38.5	-32.0	-13.8	-51.1	-44.6	29.9	-27.0
Dollar Stop/Target Exit	-32.1	-27.8	-33.6	-20.2	-42.2	-36.7	28.0	-22.6
Time Based Exit	-34.8	-34.4	-33.4	-1.3	-54.3	-37.2	12.1	-25.9
ATR Stop/Target Exit	-54.9	-44.8	-44.9	-26.8	-65.7	-52.2	-8.0	-42.8
Grand Total	-35.5	-28.4	-31.3	-9.3	-42.4	-39.2	31.5	-22.1

Sum of Prof>$25K   Column Labels ▾

Row Labels ↓T	Ags	Curr	Energ	Metals	Rates	Softs	Stock	Grand Total
Stop & Reverse Exit	396	432	414	693	99	216	1278	3528
Dollar Stop Exit	396	308	323	485	70	178	931	2691
Dollar Target Exit	341	411	369	582	106	151	1278	3238
ATR Stop Exit	319	231	325	501	43	137	827	2383
Time Based Exit	301	221	307	555	36	146	789	2355
Dollar Stop/Target Exit	292	269	252	418	50	144	885	2310
ATR Target Exit	195	341	330	504	89	112	1125	2696
ATR Stop/Target Exit	137	193	222	393	18	106	557	1626
Grand Total	2377	2406	2542	4131	511	1190	7670	20827

Average of Return on Account | Column Labels ▾

Row Labels ↓↑	120min	360min	60min	720min	1440min	Grand Total
Stop & Reverse Exit	-29.9	3.5	-58.9	26.4	19.4	-7.9
Dollar Target Exit	-31.8	0.6	-59.6	18.2	20.1	-10.5
Dollar Stop Exit	-35.6	-4.0	-63.8	9.4	-2.1	-19.2
Dollar Stop/Target Exit	-38.8	-10.6	-64.3	-0.2	0.9	-22.6
ATR Stop Exit	-49.7	-11.1	-76.8	5.7	-3.2	-27.0
ATR Target Exit	-50.8	-11.8	-77.8	13.5	20.9	-21.2
Time Based Exit	-53.7	-15.7	-78.5	7.2	10.9	-25.9
ATR Stop/Target Exit	-69.7	-35.6	-87.7	-14.0	-6.9	-42.8
Grand Total	**-45.0**	**-10.6**	**-70.9**	**8.3**	**7.5**	**-22.1**

Sum of Prof>$25K | Column Labels ▾

Row Labels ↓↑	120min	360min	60min	720min	1440min	Grand Total
Stop & Reverse Exit	513	846	252	1008	909	3528
Dollar Target Exit	497	759	244	872	866	3238
Dollar Stop Exit	398	771	183	767	572	2691
Dollar Stop/Target Exit	382	592	188	632	516	2310
ATR Target Exit	290	606	104	831	865	2696
ATR Stop Exit	274	657	108	745	599	2383
Time Based Exit	204	549	49	795	758	2355
ATR Stop/Target Exit	127	381	37	554	527	1626
Grand Total	**2685**	**5161**	**1165**	**6204**	**5612**	**20827**

Average of Return on Account | Column Labels ▾

Row Labels ↓↑	Bollinger Band	Breakout	Momentum	Mov Avg Cross	Volatility Break	Grand Total
Stop & Reverse Exit	25.3	27.2	-46.4	-52.5	7.1	-7.9
Dollar Target Exit	20.1	22.3	-50.5	-52.7	8.3	-10.5
Dollar Stop Exit	2.6	9.7	-50.0	-54.1	-4.2	-19.2
ATR Target Exit	6.9	6.1	-58.2	-58.0	-2.7	-21.2
Dollar Stop/Target Exit	-8.3	7.8	-56.1	-54.4	-2.0	-22.6
Time Based Exit	-2.4	-15.6	-54.2	-50.5	-7.2	-25.9
ATR Stop Exit	-11.8	-0.5	-54.3	-54.5	-13.8	-27.0
ATR Stop/Target Exit	-32.2	-31.1	-67.5	-60.0	-23.1	-42.8
Grand Total	**0.0**	**3.2**	**-54.6**	**-54.6**	**-4.7**	**-22.1**

Sum of Prof>$25K | Column Labels ▾

Row Labels ↓↑	Bollinger Band	Breakout	Momentum	Mov Avg Cross	Volatility Break	Grand Total
Stop & Reverse Exit	1080	981	351	261	855	3528
Dollar Target Exit	942	1075	274	201	746	3238
ATR Target Exit	812	887	234	184	579	2696
Dollar Stop Exit	730	796	300	240	625	2691
Time Based Exit	667	622	295	289	482	2355
ATR Stop Exit	629	672	288	258	536	2383
Dollar Stop/Target Exit	560	798	209	182	561	2310
ATR Stop/Target Exit	427	451	188	176	384	1626
Grand Total	**5847**	**6282**	**2139**	**1791**	**4768**	**20827**

Figure 71- Exit Results By Market Sector, Bar Size And Entry

Type

Algo Trading Cheat Code

* In most situations, the best exit is a simple Stop & Reverse, followed by a dollar target profit exit

Part 3 - More Complicated Exits

In this section, I'll take a look at some complicated exits. More complicated exits are usually a double edged sword. Many times these exits have more parameters to "tune," which is great for creating backtests, but not necessarily great for real time performance. Remember, the more parameters to optimize, the greater the chances of curvefitting.

Trailing Exit

The trailing exit is simply an exit that trails below long positions, and vice versa for short.

InputVar4*500=	$2,500

maxpositionprofit (calculated by Tradestation)	If openpositionprofit at end of bar is below the value below, then exit
$0	($2,500)
$500	($2,000)
$1,000	($1,500)
$1,500	($1,000)
$2,000	($500)
$2,500	$0
$3,000	$500
$3,500	$1,000
$4,000	$1,500

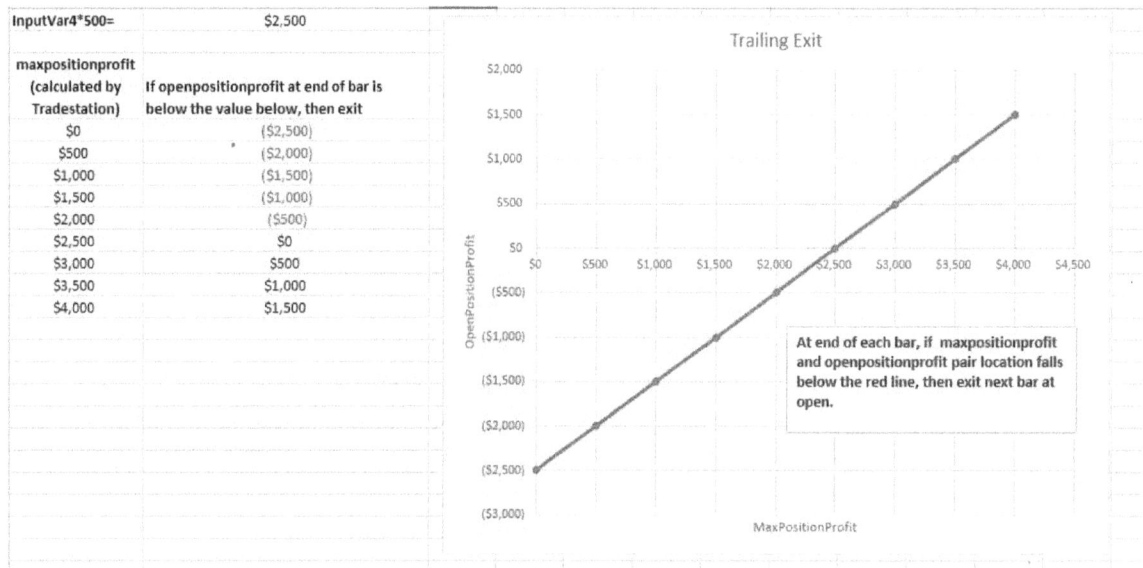

At end of each bar, if maxpositionprofit and openpositionprofit pair location falls below the red line, then exit next bar at open.

Figure 72 - Trailing Exit Definition

//trailing stop

If marketposition=1 and openpositionprofit<maxpositionprofit-InputVar4*500 then sell next bar at market;

If marketposition=-1 and openpositionprofit<maxpositionprofit-InputVar4*500 then buytocover next bar at market;

InputVar4*500 is the dollar amount you want to trail. This is not a stop order, but rather a market order that gets placed at next bar open.

The way I've written it, the condition is checked at the end of every bar.

Note that maxpositionprofit is a Tradestation keyword, and it calculates the maximum profit at any point during the open position.

You could convert this exit to a stop order if you wanted to.

So let's say you had InputVar4=5. That means the trailing level is 5*500= $2500 per contract. If maxpositionprofit never goes above $0, then when openpositionprofit (another Tradestation keyword) drops below -2500, you will get an exit signal. If maxpositionprofit hits $4000, then when openpositionprofit drops below 1500, you will get an exit signal.

Breakeven Exit

A breakeven exit is pretty simple – when the profit reaches a certain point, if the profit goes back to $0, the position is exited. This is executed using a simple Tradestation keyword:

*SetBreakEven(InputVar4*500);*

Parabolic Exit
Chandelier Exit
Yo-Yo Exit

The Parabolic, Chandelier and Yo-Yo stops are all fairly complicated exits. I won't explain them in detail here – there are plenty of good resources if you want to learn about them:

Parabolic https://www.investopedia.com/terms/p/parabolicindicator.asp

Chandelier
https://corporatefinanceinstitute.com/resources/knowledge/trading-investing/chandelier-exit/

Yo-Yo Exit

Here is a nice description of a Yo-Yo exit:

The "Yo Yo" Exit

The "Yo Yo" Exit is usually set at about 2 ATRs below the most recent close

As the close moves higher and lower the stop moves up and down – hence the name.

Logic: The "Yo Yo" exit identifies abnormal volatility in the wrong direction

The "Yo Yo" exit is a supplemental exit. It can not be your primary exit. It does not protect capital – it tells you when you are on wrong side of the market.

Figure 73 - Yo-Yo Stop In Action

Overall Results

So let's see how these 5 complicated exits perform, compared to our baseline (and current champion) Stop & Reverse Exit. Remember, the Stop & Reverse is in all the strategies, so the complicated exits will not take the place of Stop & Reverse, but will hopefully exit at more appropriate times than the Stop & Reverse exit.

Row Labels	Average of Return on Account		Row Labels	Sum of Prof>$25K
Stop & Reverse Exit	-7.9		Stop & Reverse Exit	3528
Breakeven Exit	-11.8		Breakeven Exit	3084
Trailing Exit	-24.1		Trailing Exit	2196
Parabolic Exit	-26.0		Parabolic Exit	2187
Chandelier Exit	-41.8		Chandelier Exit	1404
Yo-Yo Exit	-41.9		Yo-Yo Exit	1360
Grand Total	-25.6		Grand Total	13759

Figure 74 - Results, More Complicated Exits

Results for these more complicated exits are grouped into 3 categories. First, there is the "good" group, which has a single constituent - the Breakeven Exit. It is not much worse than the Stop & Reverse Exit. The next group has the Trailing Exit and the Parabolic Exit, with performance definitely a step down from the Breakeven Exit. The Chandelier Exit and Yo-Yo Exit are in the worst performing group.

These different levels of performance (good, average, poor) can also be seen in a comparison chart of all the exits so far:

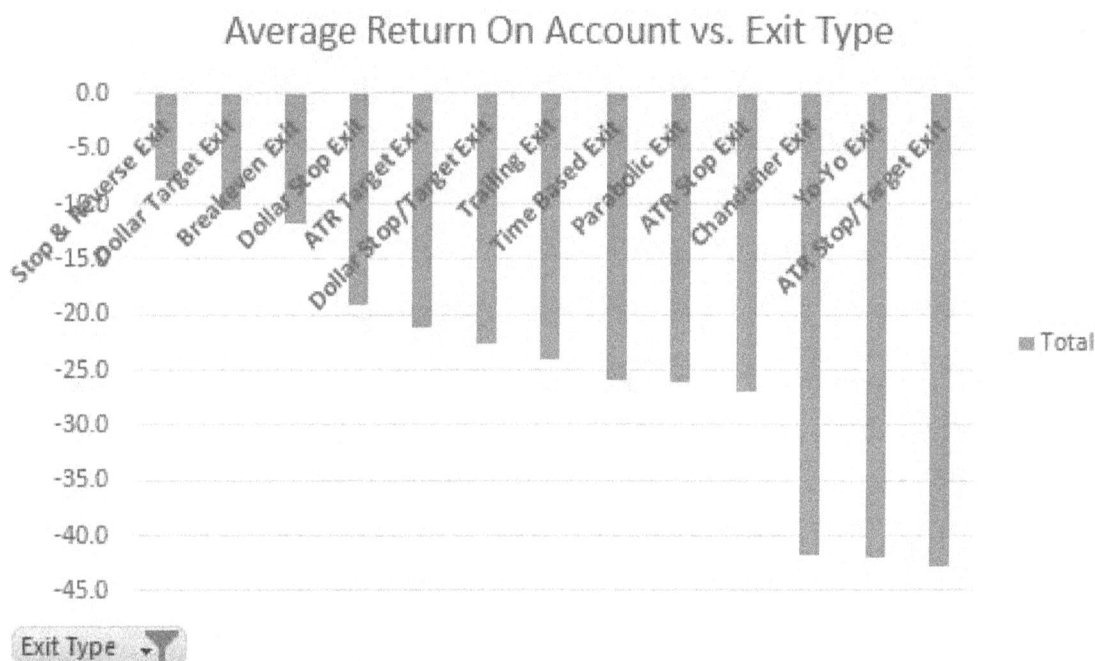

Figure 75 - Average Return, Complicated Exits

Results can be summarized as follows:

Stop & Reverse Exit is still the best.
Breakeven Stops are almost as good as Stop & Reverse.

These results hold true regardless of market sector (Stop & Reverse and Breakeven are always the best two), bar size or entry. The results and conclusions are pretty consistent.

One other interesting note here is that the smaller breakeven stop thresholds ($500 - $1000) tend to perform better. But overall the Stop & Reverse still is better than the Breakeven stop.

Algo Trading Cheat Code:
First Try Stop & Reverse Exits, Then Try Breakeven Exits

Up until this point, all the exits used have been based in part on the entry signal. The stops I have examined are based on dollars and ATRs, and use the trade entry price or bar to determine the actual level.

What about exits that did not care about the trade entry? In other words, exits based on their own calculations? Can they beat out Stop & Reverse? I'll examine that in Part 4.

Part 4 - 2 Technical Indicator Type Exits

For all the exits so far (except for Stop & Reverse and Yo-Yo), the exits were tied in some way to the entry price. The Breakeven stop, for example, is set based on the entry price, and the profit and loss from that point. So are all the dollar and ATR stops and targets. And the parabolic and chandelier stops, while incorporating price action in them, are still based on the conditions when the trade begins.

Well, maybe the best time to exit has no relationship to when you enter. Possibly, a good exit can be determined based on analysis of price itself - simple technical levels, indicators, etc. Many traders use support and resistance lines, for example, to exit.

Of course, looking at technical indicators for exiting opens the door to an unlimited array of exits - every entry you can think of could instead function purely as an exit.

Back in 2017, I hosted a weekend retreat for an advanced group of traders in Cleveland, Ohio. One group activity was to build entries and exits. And one of the findings was that "entries as exits" worked pretty well - usually better than standard run of the mill stop and target type exits.

Based on those findings by advanced traders, for this section I'll try 2 simple and popular, yet usually effective, exits based on technical indicators/price action:

Channel Exit
Simply exit long positions on the next bar if the lowest low of the last X bars is hit. Vice versa for short positions.

Moving Average Exit

When in a long position, if the close crosses below the X bar moving average, exit the long position. Vice versa for short.

I chose these 2 "entries as exits" because they are pretty common, and easy to implement. Obviously, I just scratched the surface with this concept, so I'll leave it to the reader to take the next steps with the idea.

Overall Results

Row Labels	Average of Return on Account
Stop & Reverse Exit	-7.9
Channel Exit	-36.1
Mov Avg Exit	-44.7
Grand Total	-29.5

Figure 76 - Standard Technical Indicators As Exits

Yuck!

These exits are nowhere near as good as Stop & Reverse. So, rather than bore you with details of the results, I'll just stop here. The Channel & Moving Average Exits - at least how I tested them - are not that good.

Here are the results for Return on Account and Cases With Profit > $25K, for all 15 of the tested exits.

Average Return On Account vs. Exit Type

Profitable Cases > $25K vs. Exit Type

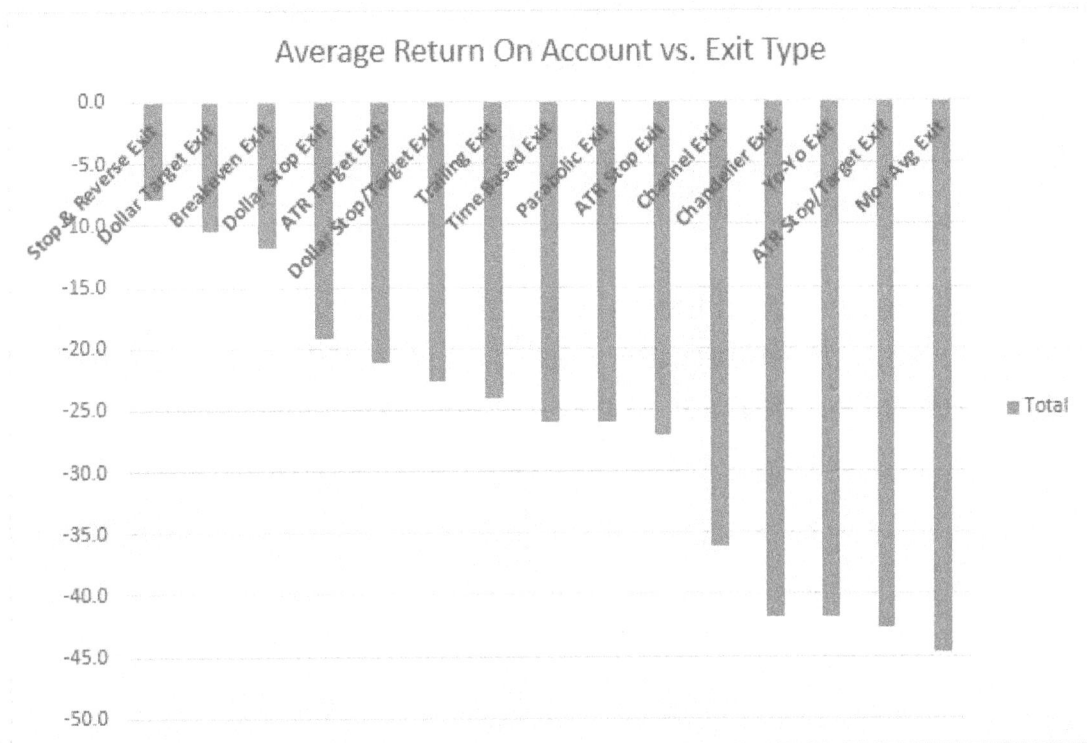

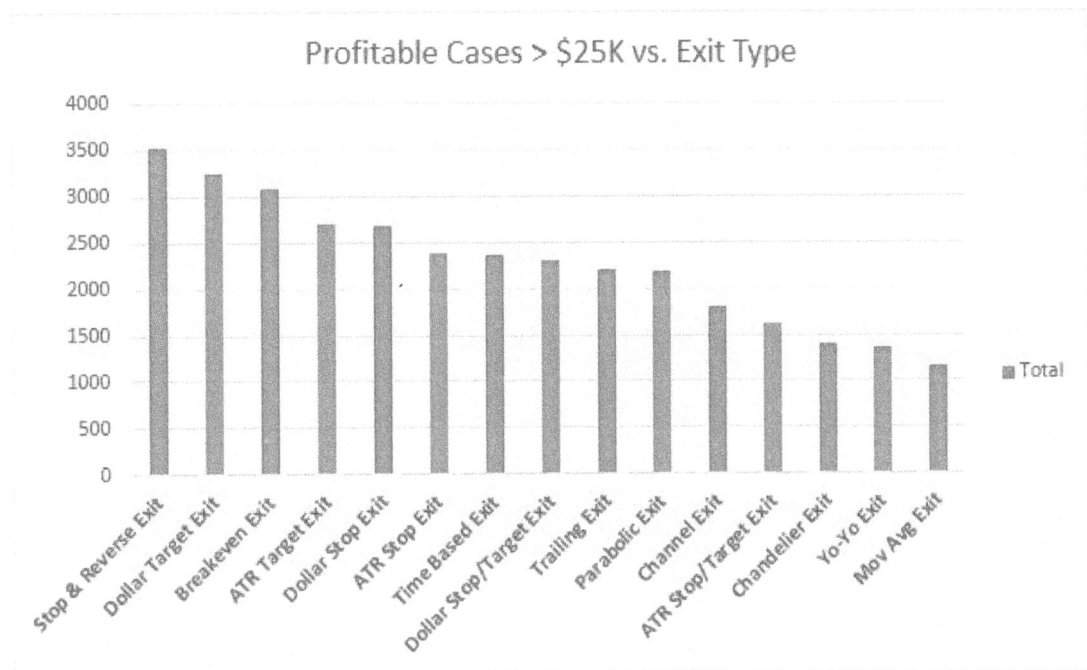

Figure 77 - Using Technical Indicators As Exits

This has been an interesting study so far, but also a bit depressing. I thought for sure something - anything! - would beat the simple Stop & Reverse Exit. Yet nothing has!

Maybe my results are a fluke, a testament to keeping strategies simple. Maybe you'll get different results in your testing.

Algo Trading Cheat Code:

* Technically Based Exits – Exits that are independent of the entry or the current position profit/loss, are worth testing. Although, the two I tested for this chapter did not beat the Stop & Reverse exit

CHAPTER 9 – REWARD TO RISK STUDY

Is There An "Optimum" Reward To Risk Ratio?

The Internet is a great place to argue with complete strangers, isn't it? Ugh, I hate when that happens! Although I try to avoid conflicts, I'll admit to a few Internet tussles over the years. It usually never works out well for anyone involved, so nowadays I try my best to avoid them.

I was reminded of my past Internet arguments (all of which I won, LOL) the other day when I saw a provocative thread at a trading forum: "Optimum Reward/Risk."

Immediately upon seeing this I went into "fight" mode, because in my experience, there really is no best Reward to Risk (or Risk To Reward, as some people refer to it). Rather, the optimum result is something specific to the particular market or strategy being tested.

And if you have picked up anything from this book yet, it is that I am all for testing. Don't rely on anyone (including me!) to tell you what is best in trading. Instead, "listen and trust, but always verify." This means you might like what I say, think I'm a nice guy and value my trading experience, but you'll STILL verify what I tell you – with your own testing.

There is no better way of getting confidence in what you are trading then by testing and verifying it yourself.

So, back to the trading forum thread…

The poster concluded that a reward to risk ratio of 3-4 to 1 was best. This means if your stop loss is $1,000, you should have a profit target of $3,000 to $4,000. He backed up his claim with a very nice and well thought out study. My biggest issue with the study was that he used simulated data, not actual market data.

Based on my experience, I had doubts about his conclusion. As a result, I decided to test it myself, as I always do. In this chapter I try to answer the question:

"Is there a 'best' Reward:Risk ratio when entering randomly, but exiting with X ATR profit or Y ATR stop?"

Study Setup

I decided to test a random entry approach with stop losses and profit targets, using 10 years of Daily data (from 2011-2021), for 7 futures markets:

Crude Oil (energies)

Cotton (softs)

Euro Currency (currencies)

Mini S&P (Stock Indices)

Gold (metals)

10 Year Treasury Notes (rates)

Soybeans (ags)

This is a nice cross section of market sectors. As far as bar size, I used Daily bars since I felt lower timeframes would suffer too much from the slippage and commission costs, which (of course) I included in this study.

I'll be the first to say that different markets could produce different results (they probably do), and different bar sizes might also produce different results. Since I provide all code in Tradestation Easy Language format, the reader can fairly easily tailor this strategy for his or her own needs.

Pseudo Code

If there is no current open market position (you are flat), flip a coin to see if you have a trade for the next bar. Heads means take a trade at open of next bar. Tails means stay flat.

Now, if there is a trade indicated for the next day, flip the coin again. If it is heads, the trade direction is long. If tails, the trade should be short.

Of course, you can change these random percentages – you don't have to use a coin! – if you desire.

Once you are in a trade, there is a stop loss and a profit target. Both are based on the 15 period Average True Range, multiplied by an adjustable value. Profit targets are assumed to be hit only if the price is exceeded by one tick. No inaccurate "touch fills" here.

For bookkeeping purposes, any open trades are closed out at the end of the test period.

Tradestation Code
Strategy: KJD2021-02 ExitRandom 01
Workspace: 2020-02 Random

input:
outputfile("C:\Users\Trader\Documents\Futures\FinalTYfast.txt"),iter(1),PT(2
var:posstradetoday(0),NProf(0),NLoss(0),markpos(0),FFAOK(True);

posstradetoday=random(1); //random number for today's trade

If posstradetoday<=oddstradetoday and marketposition=0 then begin //trade will occur today

//enter trade
If random(1)<percentlong then buy next bar at open
Else sellshort next bar at open;

end;

*setStopLoss(SL*AvgTrueRange(15)*BigPointValue);*
*setProfitTarget(PT*AvgTrueRange(15)*BigPointValue);*

If LastBarOnChart then begin
Sell this bar at close;
BuyToCover this bar at close;
End;

//print out statistics to file (could modify to print to print log)
//IMPORTANT: Use compatibility mode for FastFileAppend

if LastBaronChart and GetAppInfo(aiOptimizing) = 1 then begin
FFAOK = FastFileAppend(OutPutFile, NumToStr(PT, 1) + "," +

NumToStr(SL, 1) + "," + NumToStr(NetProfit, 2) + ","

+ NumToStr(100*NumWinTrades/TotalTrades, 2) + ","+
NumToStr(TotalTrades, 2)+ ","+ NumToStr(
NetProfit/(TotalTrades+.000001),2)+ ","

+NumToStr(-5-((-.125*(100*NumWinTrades/TotalTrades))+25), 3
)+ ","

+NumToStr((NetProfit/(TotalTrades+.000001))-5-((-.125*
(100*NumWinTrades/TotalTrades))+25), 3)+ ","

+NumToStr(TotalTrades*((NetProfit/(TotalTrades+.000001))-5-
((-.125*(100*NumWinTrades/TotalTrades))+25)), 3)+ ","

+NumToStr(PT/SL, 3)

+ newLine) ;

end ;

To get enough data, I am running each combination of stop loss (SL) and profit target (PT) 5,000 times. I am running 14 different values of PT, from 0.5 to 7.0 in steps of 0.5. I am also doing this with stop losses.

All together, there are 980,000 random backtests for each symbol, or 6,860,000 backtests total.

```
iters=1 to 5000
PT=.5 to 7 step .5
SL=.5 to 7 step .5
```

With the PT and SL values I chose, the various combinations produce reward to risk values of 0.071 to 14.0, which is a wide range to examine. For small PT and SL values, I made sure to use Look Inside Bar Backtesting to ensure accurate results.

I should point out a "pet peeve" of mine with reward to risk. Many times I have heard someone (usually a new trader) say "I like a risk reward ratio of 3. That way, I win $3 for $1 I lose."

That's totally backwards! Risk:Reward in that case is 1:3. So, you will see me referring to Reward:Risk or Re:Ri just to eliminate any confusion. Just put the reward amount first, and "Reward to Risk" will be the right thing to say.

Results – Sanity Check

Whenever I run big studies, I am always worried about screwing something up and getting misleading results. So, when I can, I like to run what I call a "sanity check" – do my results make sense?

If this random entry is truly working, without slippage and commissions when I have a reward to risk of 1, I should have a winning percentage of 50%. If I have a reward to risk of 3:1, I should win 25% of the time, and conversely a reward:risk of 0.333 should equate to a 75% win rate.

When I look at the results (again, this is without slippage and commissions) these values match the random simulation output. Therefore, the "sanity check" is passed!

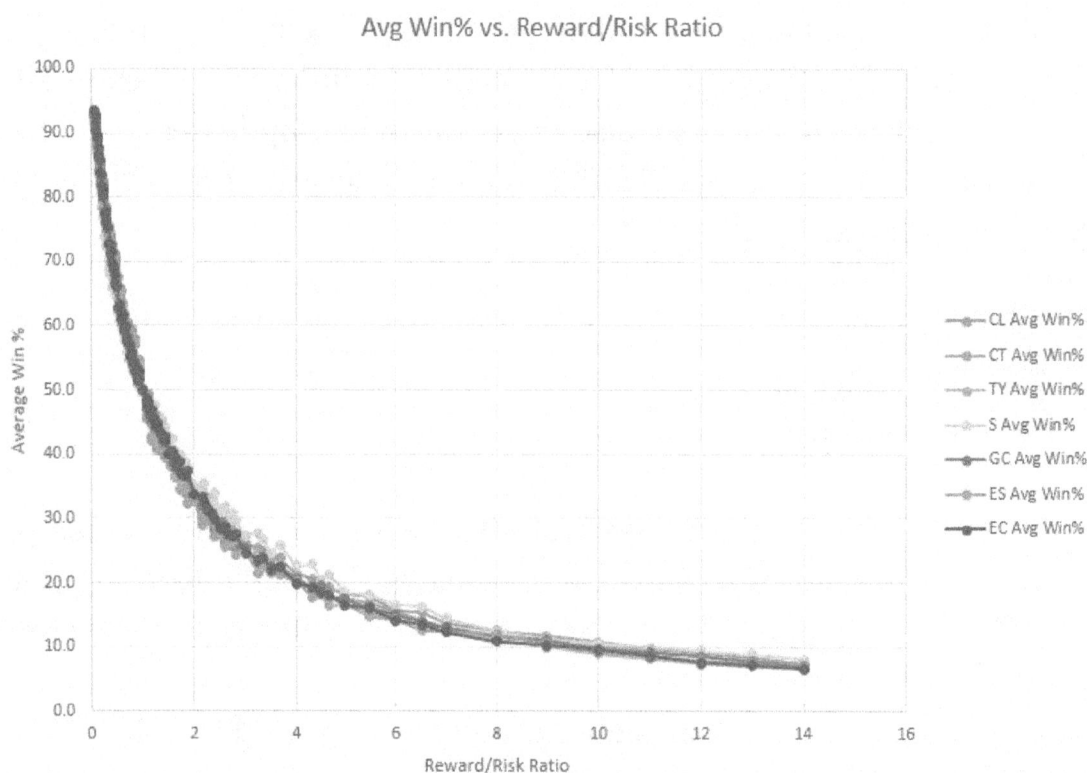

Figure 78 - Sanity Check For Reward/Risk Study

Detailed Results - ES

Let's see what kind of results we get with ES, after including slippage and commissions:

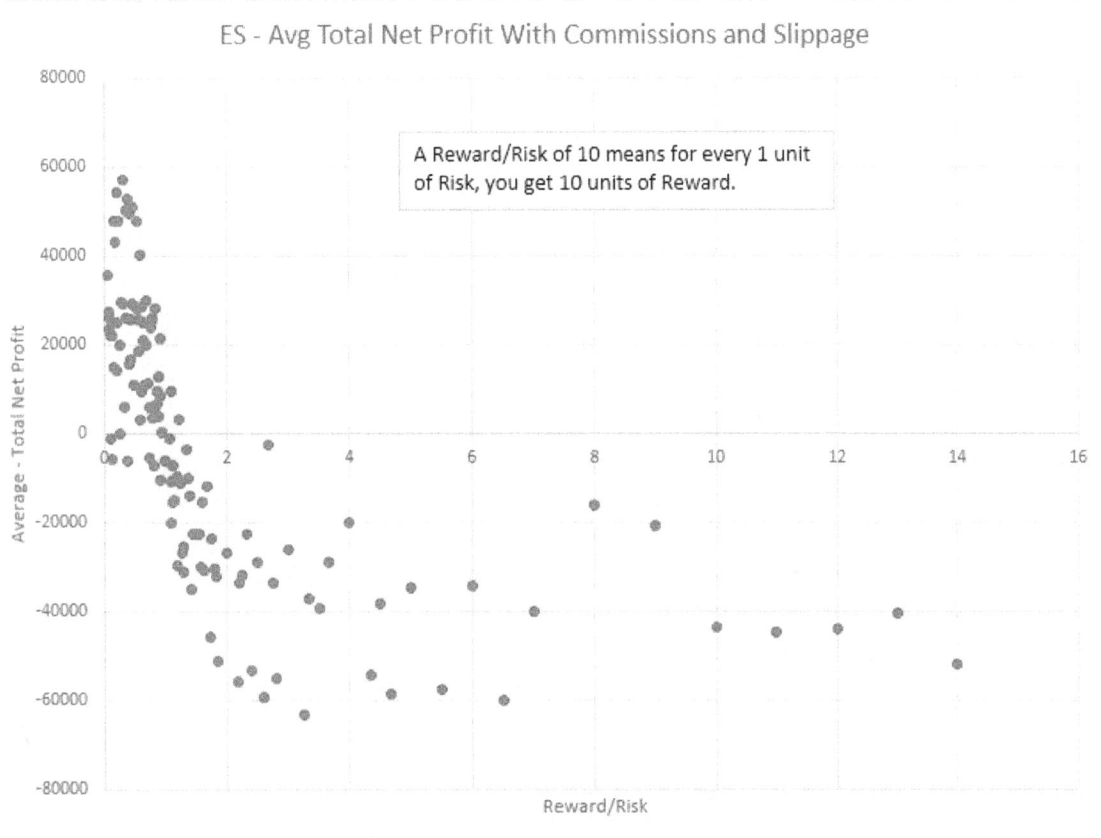

Figure 79 - Reward/Risk Results, ES

These results are interesting! They tell us that small profit targets with larger stop losses are the best. In fact, the best overall Profit Target is 1.0 ATR, with the best stop loss of 7.0 ATR. Clearly nowhere near the "common wisdom" best reward:risk of 3!

ES - PT - in ATRs with S&C

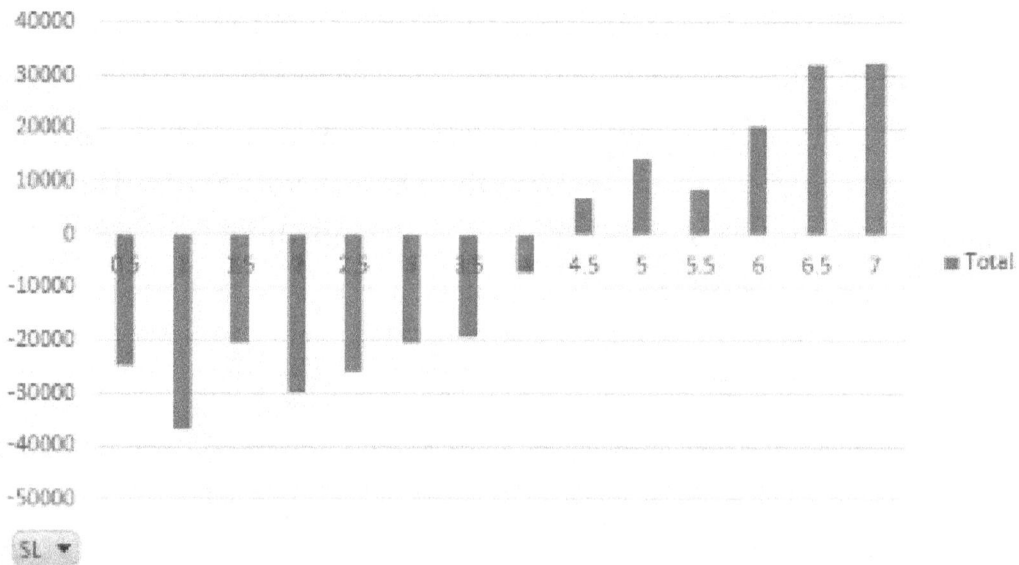

ES - SL - in ATRs with S&C

Figure 80- ES Reward/Risk Results

Detailed Results – GC, TY, CT, EC

Let's see what kind of results we get with GC (Gold), TY (10 Year Notes), CT (cotton) and EC (Euro Currency). I include all these together because their reward to risk profile is basically the same. The best reward:risk is always under 1.

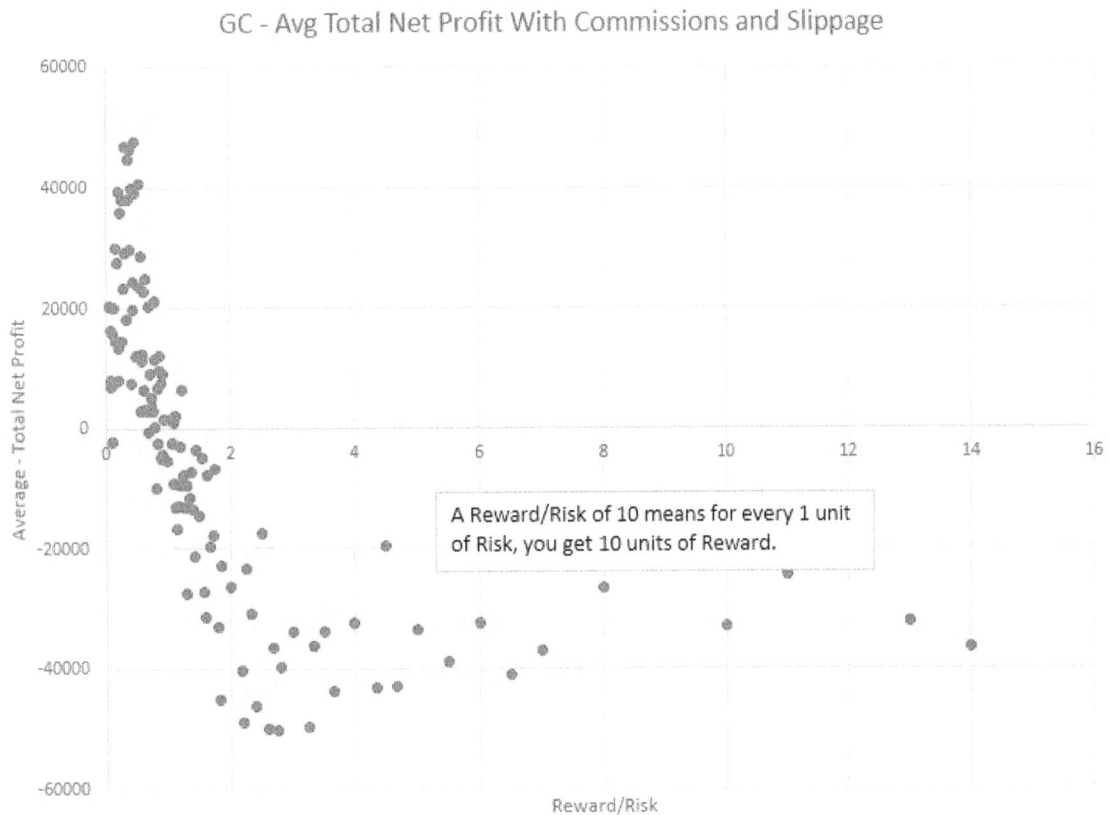

GC - Avg Total Net Profit With Commissions and Slippage

A Reward/Risk of 10 means for every 1 unit of Risk, you get 10 units of Reward.

Figure 81 - Gold, Reward/Risk Results

Again, from 980,000 backtests, the best results are with a reward to risk of much less than 1.0.

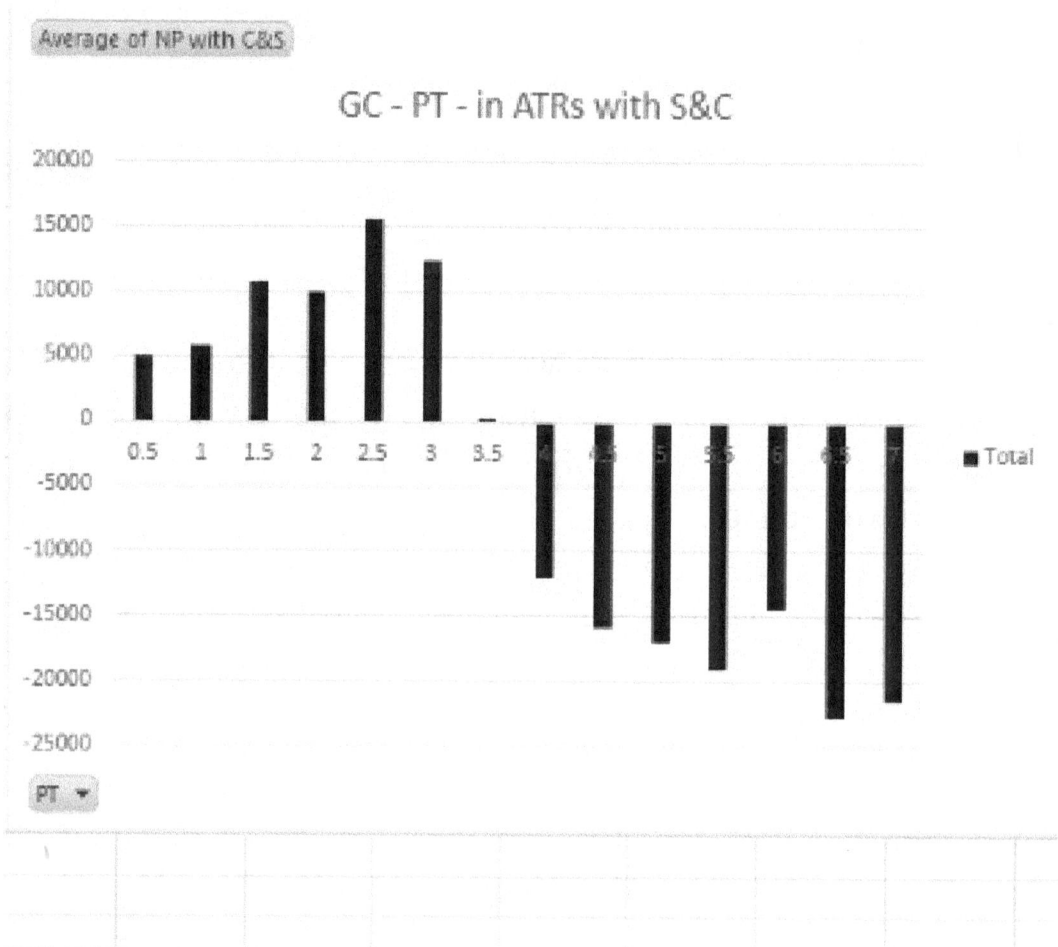

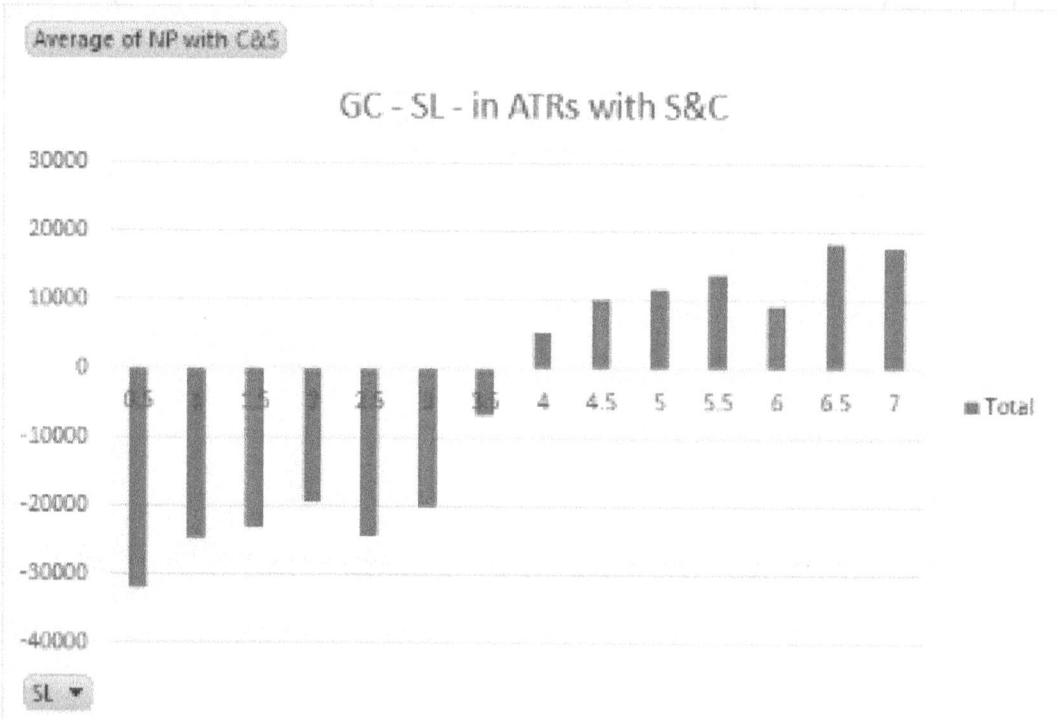

Figure 82 - Gold, Reward/Risk Results

TY - Avg Total Net Profit With Commissions and Slippage

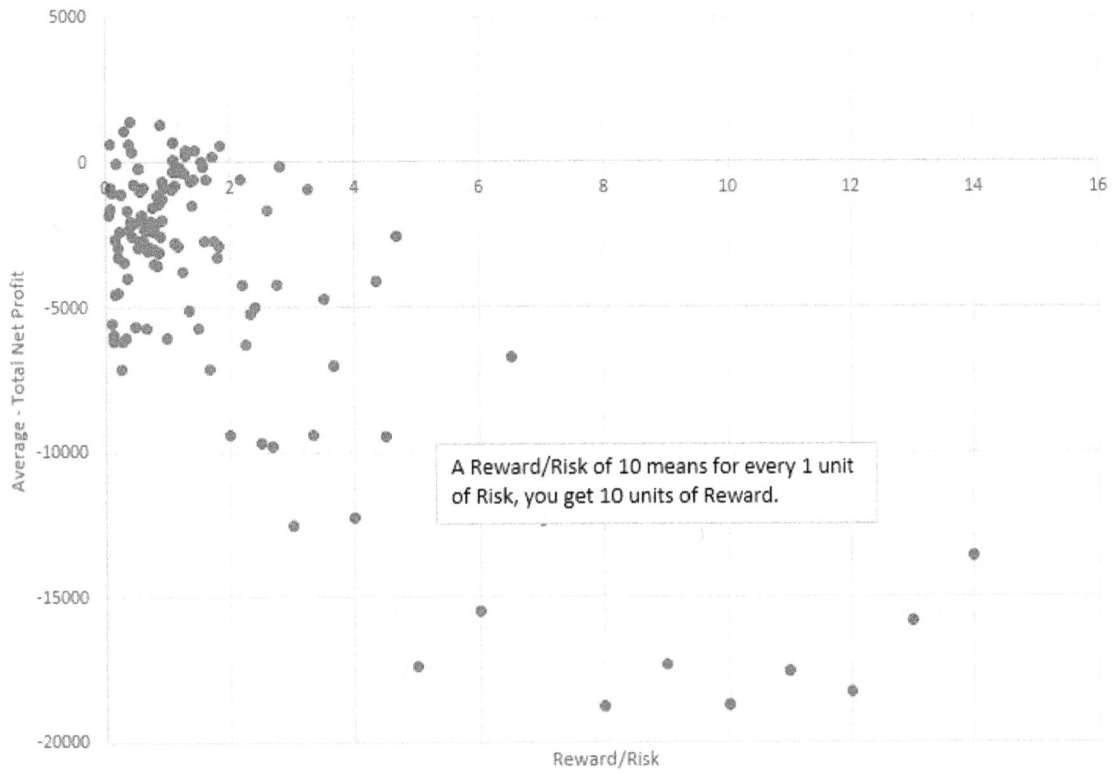

A Reward/Risk of 10 means for every 1 unit of Risk, you get 10 units of Reward.

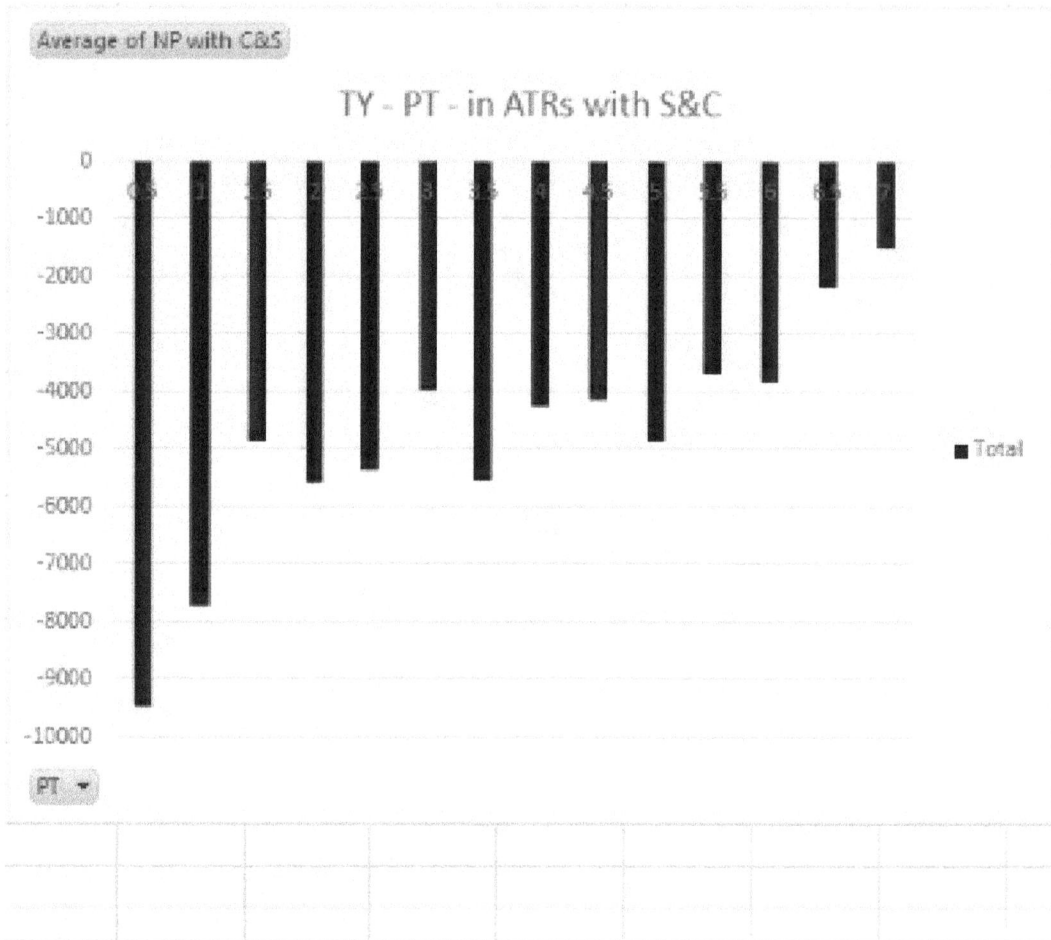

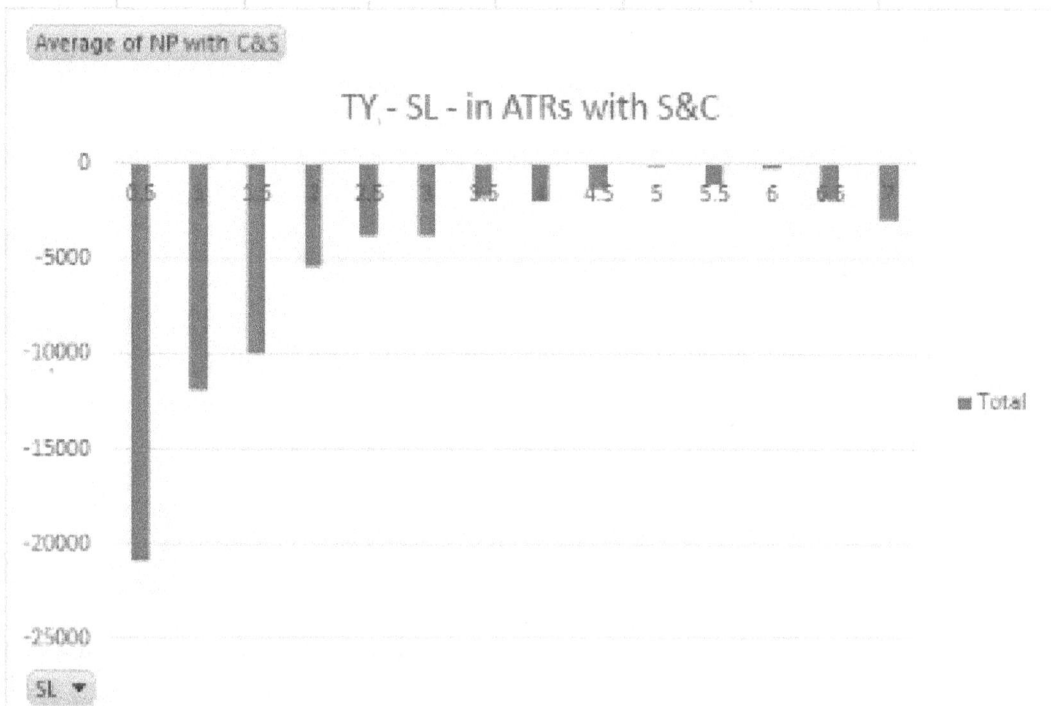

Figure 83 - 10 Year Notes, Reward/Risk Results

CT - Avg Total Net Profit With Commissions and Slippage

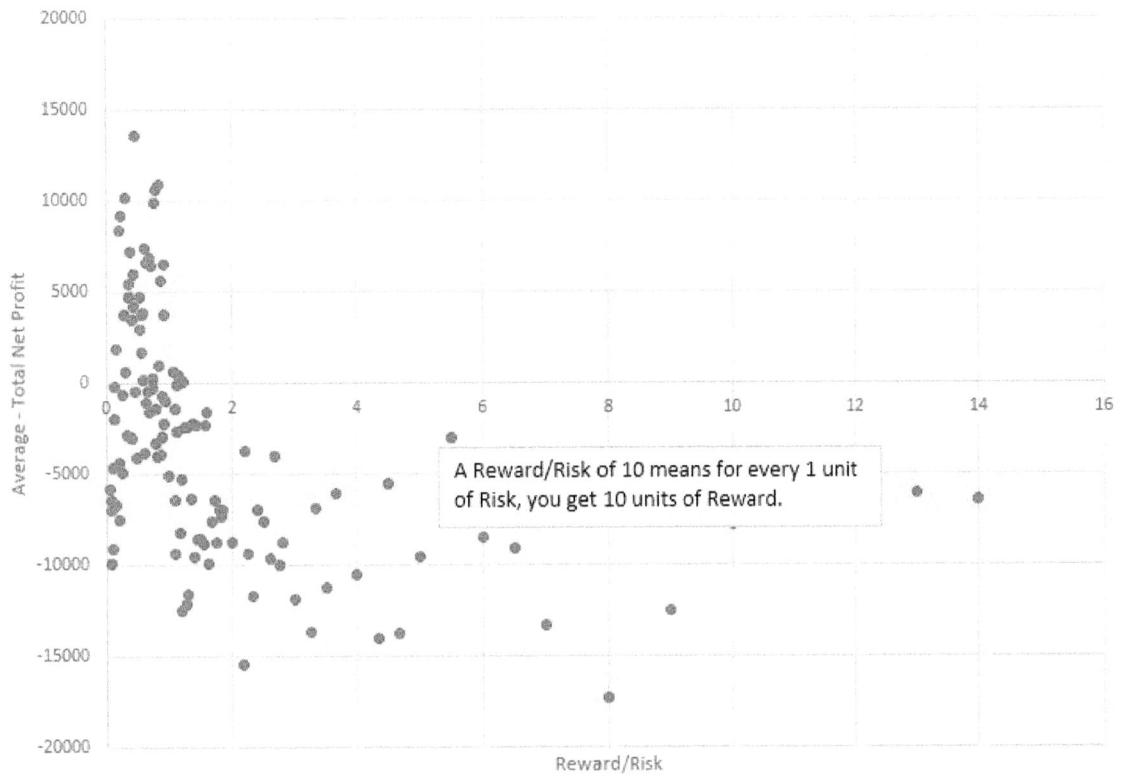

A Reward/Risk of 10 means for every 1 unit of Risk, you get 10 units of Reward.

Average of NP with C&S

CT - PT - in ATRs with S&C

PT ▾

Average of NP with C&S

CT - SL - in ATRs with S&C

SL ▾

Figure 84 - Cotton, Reward/Risk Results

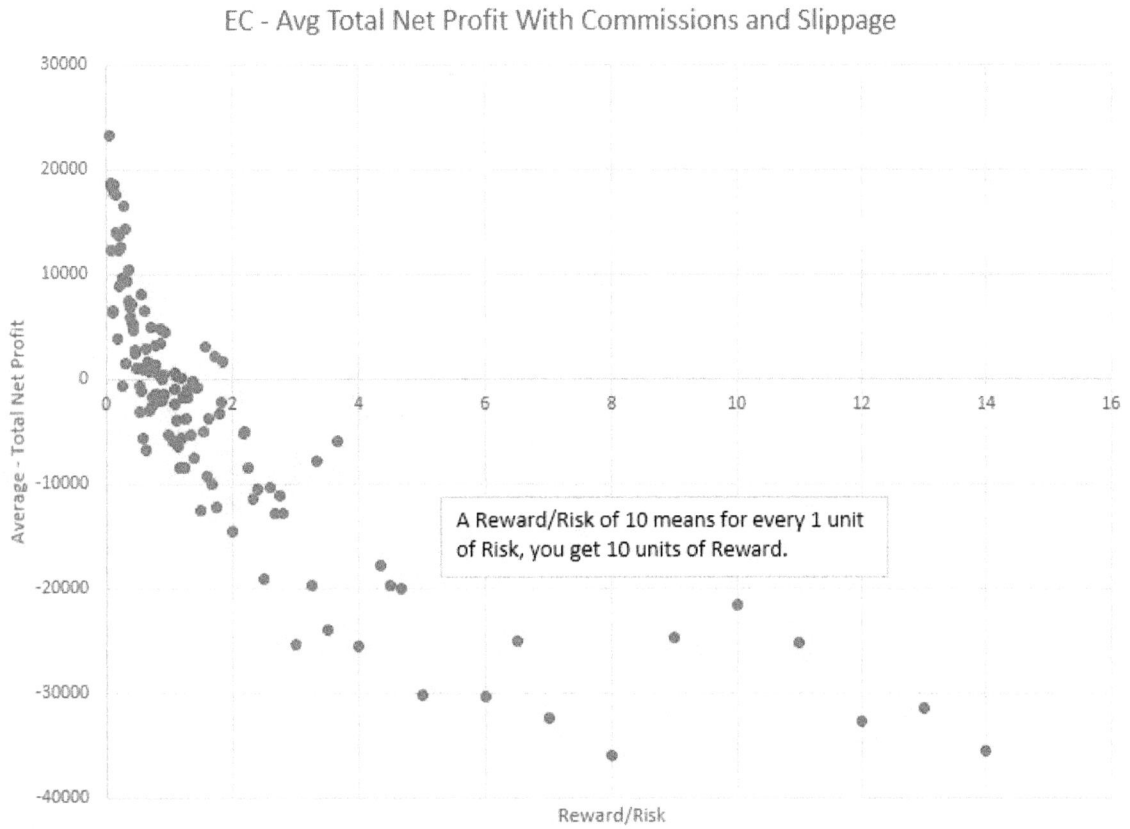

EC - Avg Total Net Profit With Commissions and Slippage

A Reward/Risk of 10 means for every 1 unit of Risk, you get 10 units of Reward.

EC - PT - in ATRs with S&C

PT ▼

Average of NP with C&S

EC - SL - in ATRs with S&C

SL ▼

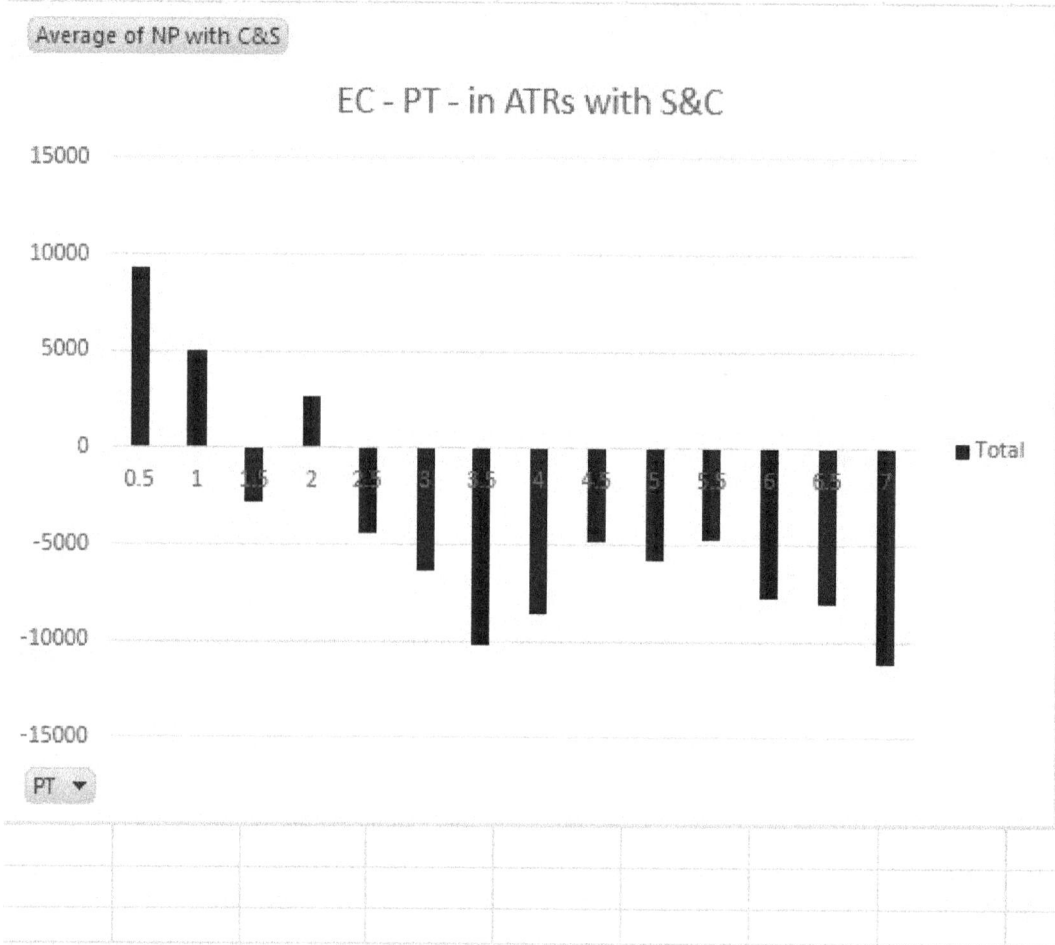

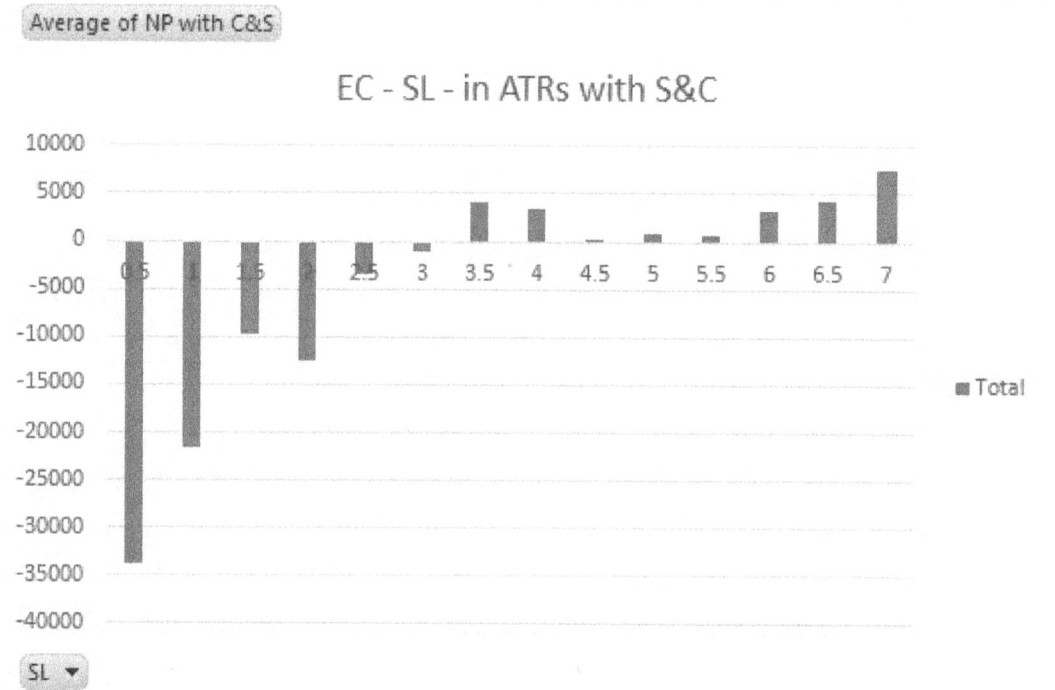

Figure 85 - Euro Currency, Reward/Risk Results

Detailed Results S and CL

So far, we have five markets and market sectors that all show a reward to risk of below 1 is optimum, for a random entry test. Clearly not what I expected, but as I've said many, many (too many!) times "you have to test!" You might stop here and conclude "a reward:risk below 1 is optimum." But why stop here?

Now, let's throw a wrench in this analysis, and show you S (Soybeans) and Crude Oil (CL). The results, shown in the charts that follow, actually have an optimum reward to risk around 3 to 4. In other words, a totally different outcome than the 5 other markets!

S - Avg Total Net Profit With Commissions and Slippage

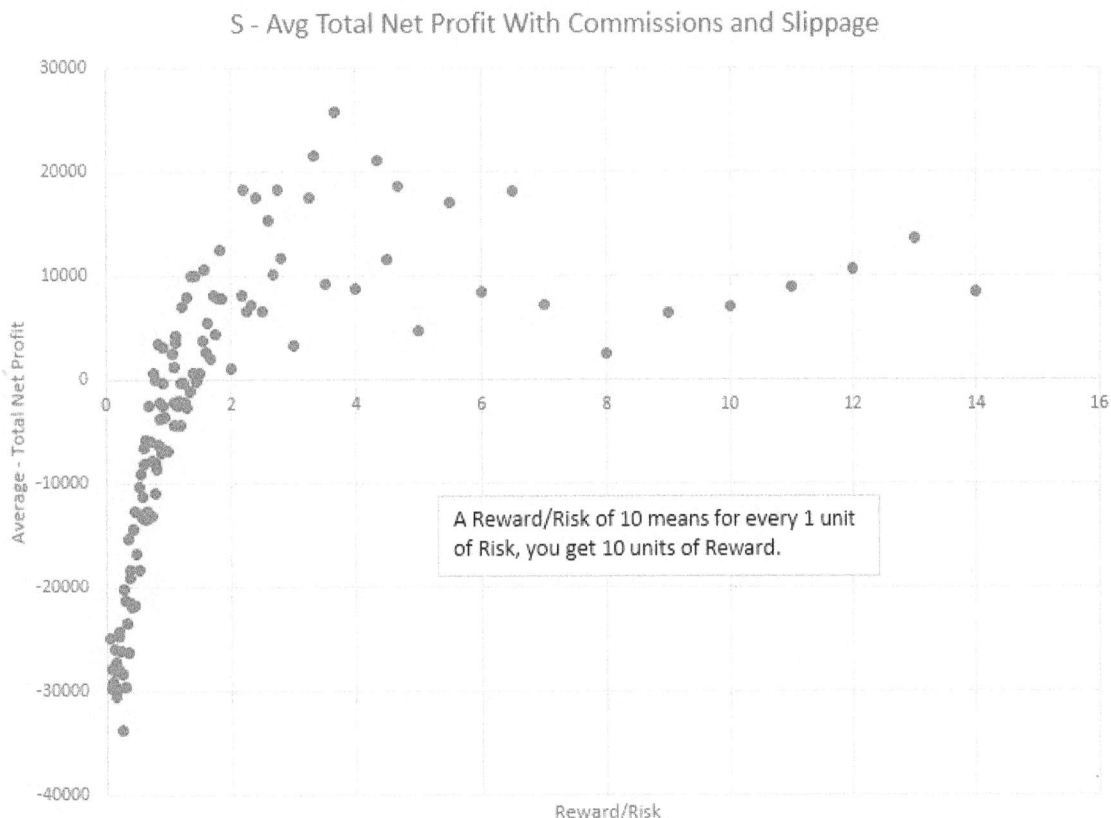

A Reward/Risk of 10 means for every 1 unit of Risk, you get 10 units of Reward.

S - PT - in ATRs with S&C

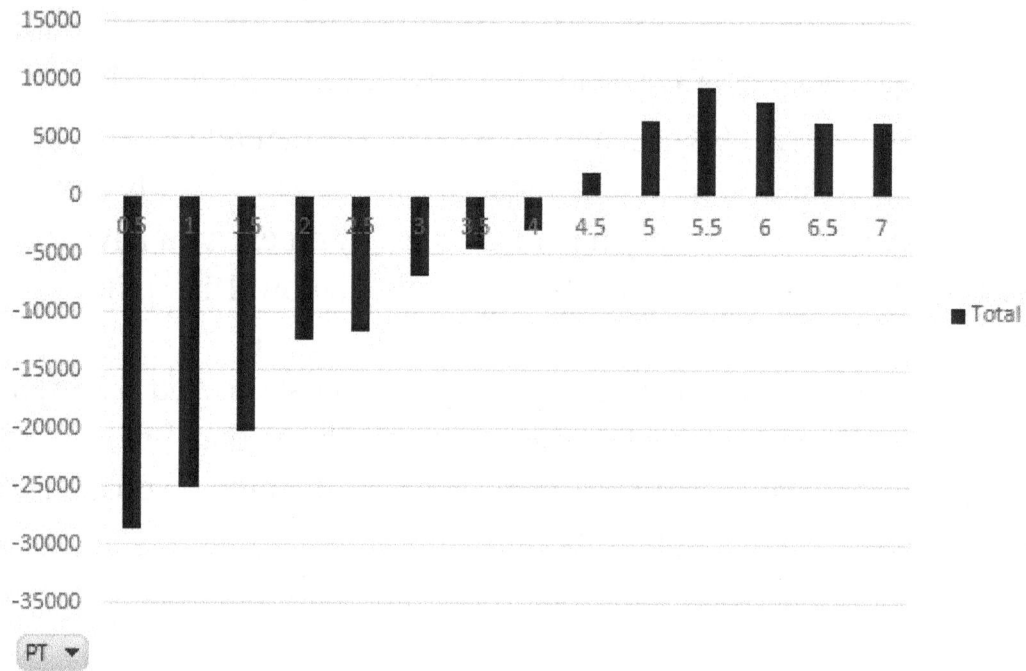

PT ▾

S - SL - in ATRs with S&C

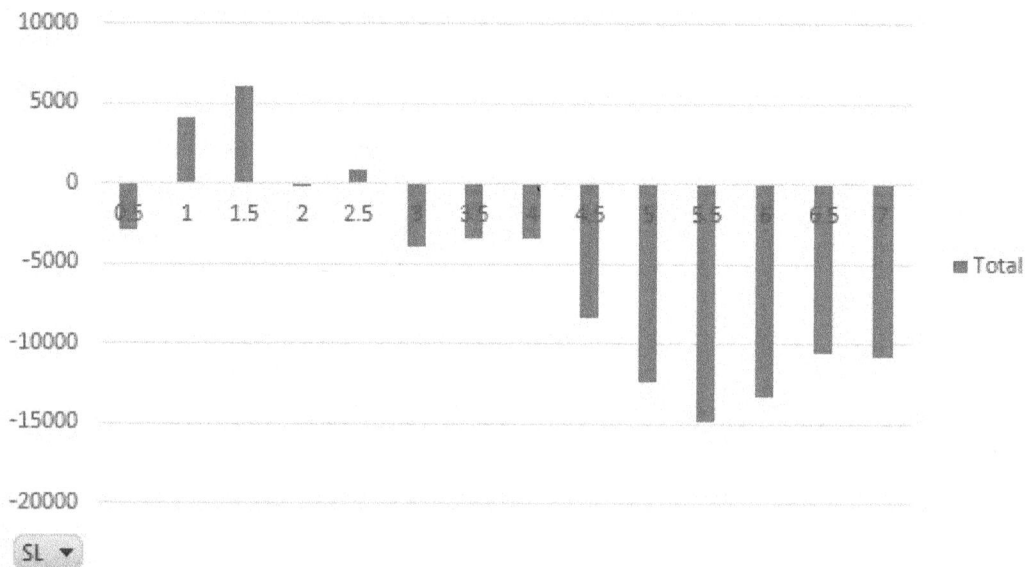

SL ▾

Figure 86 - Soybeans Reward/Risk Results

CL - Avg Total Net Profit With Commissions and Slippage

A Reward/Risk of 10 means for every 1 unit of Risk, you get 10 units of Reward.

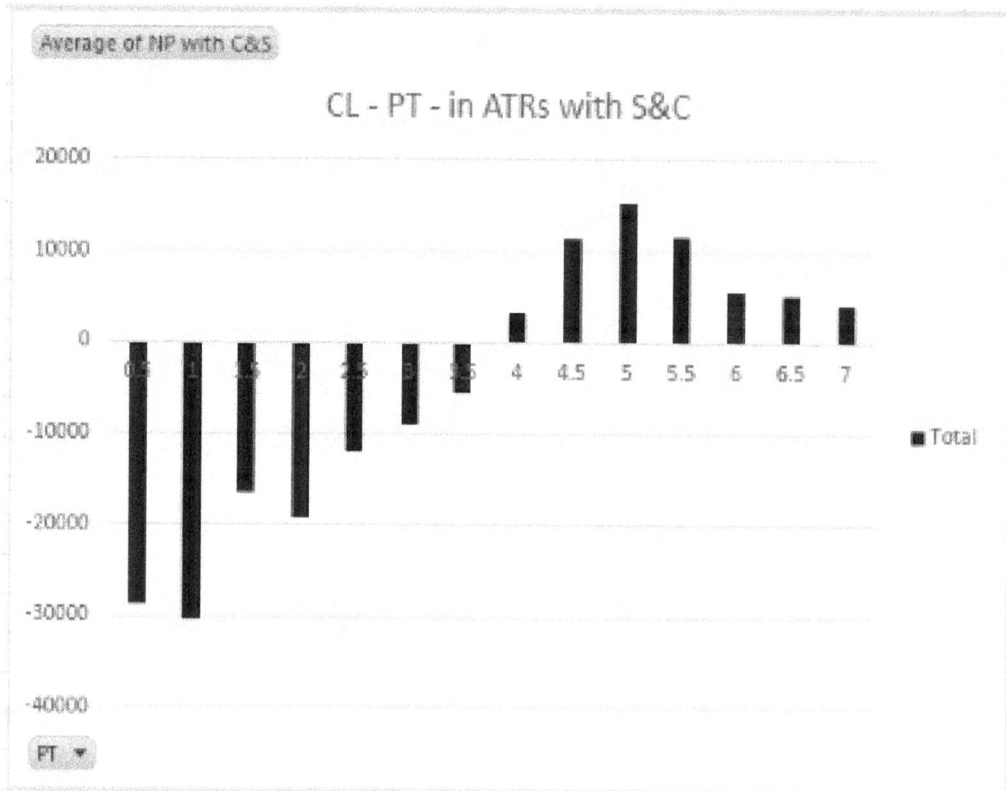

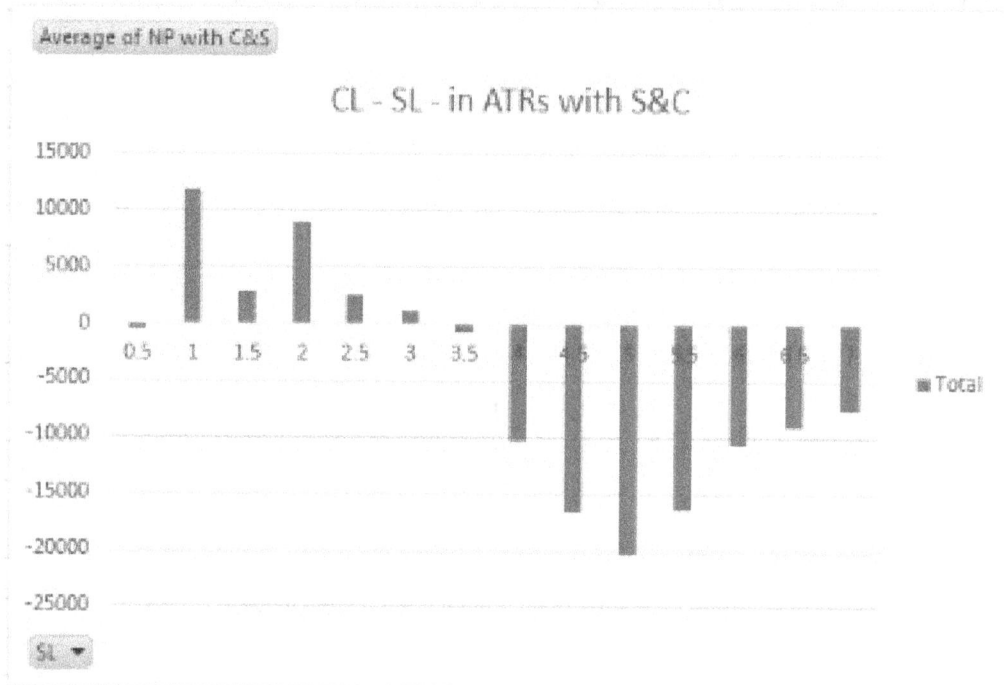

Figure 87 - Crude Oil - Reward/Risk Results

Summary Of Results

Market	Best Re:Ri	Best Prof ATR	Best Loss ATR	Chance Win with Best Prof/Loss ATR
ES	0.3	2	7	89.4%
GC	0.5	2.5	6.5	78.1%
TY	0.4	7 (LOSER)	6.5 (LOSER)	48.6%
CT	0.5	3	6.5	31.6%
EC	0.1	.5	7	78.9%
S	3.7	5.5	1.5	79.0%
CL	2.75	5	1	69.1%

The best reward to risk for most markets I tested was well under 1. But 2 markets were optimum around 3-4 reward to risk. So much for market adages!

I should remind you that this study is for Daily bars only. It is possible that other size bars will yield completely different results.

Algo Trading Cheat Codes

* There is no universal optimum Reward to Risk ratio
* If you use profit targets and stop losses in your strategy, consider running a random entry study like this first, to help you decide how to set the Reward:Risk
* If you test very small profit targets and stop losses – where both could be hit on the same bar – make sure you use Look Inside Bar Backtesting or Bar Magnifier, depending on your software. Otherwise your results could be

incorrect

* This study shows you MIGHT be able to make money trading a random entry strategy! Look at the table above, the far right column. It says if you ran a random entry strategy for ES with a 2.0 PT and 7.0 ATR, you'd actually have a 89.4% chance of ending up with a profit! I don't necessarily recommend it, but it is food for thought…

CHAPTER 10 – PROFITABLE CLOSES STUDY

Is Exiting After "X" Profitable Closes A Good Idea?

Continuing the research I conducted in the previous chapter, I decided to examine if there was any benefit to exiting after a specified number of profitable bars, or exiting after a specified number of non-profitable bars.

This is based on a concept put forth by trading legend Larry Williams. In his most popular version, he'd exit a position at the next open after the first profitable close.

I decided to expand on that study by looking at 1 to 10 profitable bars before closing the position, and also 1 to 10 non-profitable bars before closing.

Note that this does not mean consecutive profitable bars, or even bars of increasing profitability. For example, if you wanted to exit after the second profitable bar, and the first bar profit was +$100, and the second bar lost $5, you'd still exit, since the trade encountered the 2nd profitable closing bar (with the 2nd close having a $95 profit).

I'll leave it to the reader to explore these other variations:
- X consecutive profitable bars
- X profitable bars of increasing profit each bar
- X consecutive profitable bars of increasing profit each bar

So this study focuses on one question: Is there a "best" NProfitable closes value when entering randomly, exiting either after X profitable closes or Y non-profitable closes?

Study Setup

I decided to test a random entry approach with stop losses and profit targets, using 10 years of Daily data (from 2011-2021), for 7 futures markets:

Crude Oil (energies)

Cotton (softs)

Euro Currency (currencies)

Mini S&P (stock indices)

Gold (metals)
10 Year Treasury Notes (rates)
Soybeans (ags)

I'll be the first to say that different markets could produce different results (they probably do), and different bar sizes might also produce different results. Since I provide all code in Tradestation Easy Language format, the reader can fairly easily tailor this strategy for his or her own research needs.

Pseudo Code

If there is no current open market position (you are flat), flip a coin to see if you have a trade for the next bar. Heads means take a trade at open of next bar. Tails means stay flat.

Now, if there is a trade indicated for the next day, flip the coin again. If it is heads, the trade direction is long. If tails, the trade should be short.

Of course, you can change these random entry percentages – you don't have to use a 50/50 coin! – if you desire.

Once you are in a trade, there is a profit based exit and a loss based exit. Both are based on reaching the input value of number of profitable closes, or number of non-profitable closes. These represent 2 inputs that will be varied as part of the test.

For bookkeeping purposes, any open trades are closed out at the end of the test.

Tradestation Code

input:
OutPutFile("C:\Users\Trader\Documents\Futures\NProfES.txt"),iter(1),NNPr
  var:posstradetoday(0),NProf(0),NLoss(0),markpos(0) ,FFAOK(True);

posstradetoday=random(1); //random number for today's trade

If posstradetoday<=oddstradetoday and marketposition=0 then begin

//trade will occur today

> *//enter trade*
> *If random(1)<percentlong then buy next bar at open*
> *Else sellshort next bar at open;*
> *NProf=0;*
> *NLoss=0;*
> *end;*

markpos=marketposition;

//exit after NProf profitable closes, or NLoss losing closes
If marketposition=1 and markpos[1]=1 and openpositionprofit>0 then NProf=NProf+1;
If marketposition=1 and markpos[1]=1 and openpositionprofit<0 then NLoss=NLoss+1;

If marketposition=-1 and markpos[1]=-1 and openpositionprofit>0 then NProf=NProf+1;
If marketposition=-1 and markpos[1]=-1 and openpositionprofit<0 then NLoss=NLoss+1;

If (NProf>=NNProf or NLoss>=NNLoss) and marketposition=1 then sell next bar at market;
If (NProf>=NNProf or NLoss>=NNLoss) and marketposition=-1 then buytocover next bar at market;

If marketposition=0 then begin
NProf=0;
NLoss=0;
End;

If LastBarOnChart then begin

```
Sell this bar at close;
BuyToCover this bar at close;
End;

//print(date," ",marketposition,"        ",NProf,"        ",NLoss);
var:FFAOK(True);

//IMPORTANT:  Use compatibility mode for FastFileAppend

    if LastBaronChart and GetAppInfo( aiOptimizing ) = 1 then
   begin
       FFAOK = FastFileAppend( OutputFile, NumToStr( NNProf, 1 )  +
"," + NumToStr( NNLoss, 1 ) + "," + NumToStr( NetProfit, 2 ) + ","
         + NumToStr( 100*NumWinTrades/TotalTrades, 2 ) + ","+
NumToStr(       TotalTrades,       2)+       ","+       NumToStr(
NetProfit/(TotalTrades+.000001),2 )+ ","

       +NumToStr( (NetProfit/(TotalTrades+.000001))-25, 3 )+ ","
       +NumToStr( TotalTrades*((NetProfit/(TotalTrades+.000001))-25),
3 )+ ","
       +NumToStr( NNProf/NNLoss, 2 )
       + newLine ) ;
    end ;
```

For this study, I will run each simulation 5,000 times. I will vary NProf – the number of profitable closes from 1 to 10 in steps of 1 – and I'll do the same with NLoss, the number of unprofitable closes.

This results in 500,000 backtests for each symbol, and since I am testing 7 daily bars, the end result is 3.5 million backtests in total.

```
    iters=1 to 5000
    NProf=1 to 10
    NLoss=1 to 10
```

7 markets tested, daily bars: ES, S, GC, CT, TY, CL, EC

Years tested: 2011-2021

Results

As usual, I will look only at results including commissions and slippage. I am amazed over and over by how many people (typically fraudulent trading educators) will claim that slippage is not really a thing. How wrong they are!

Think of slippage this way: if you entered a market and immediately exited, what would be your loss? Chances are you'd lose at least 1 tick, along with commissions.

For example, let's say the ES was trading at 3930.00 bid, 3930.25 ask, with a last price of 3930.25. If you entered a "buy at market" order, you'd likely pay the ask price of 3930.25. And if you immediately exited, you'd probably receive 3930.00. So, that trade cost you 0.25 points, or 1 tick.

If you conducted a strategy backtest of this trade, it would likely show an entry and exit at the same exact price. That difference between your real account and the strategy backtest is what I call slippage, and it is always there. It is the price you pay to trade in the market.

For ES (mini S&P), this NProf/NLoss approach isn't very profitable with a random entry strategy. It is quite a bit worse than the Profit Target / Stop Loss study shown earlier.

But, as with the earlier study, going for small profits and large losses seems to work the best in this market.

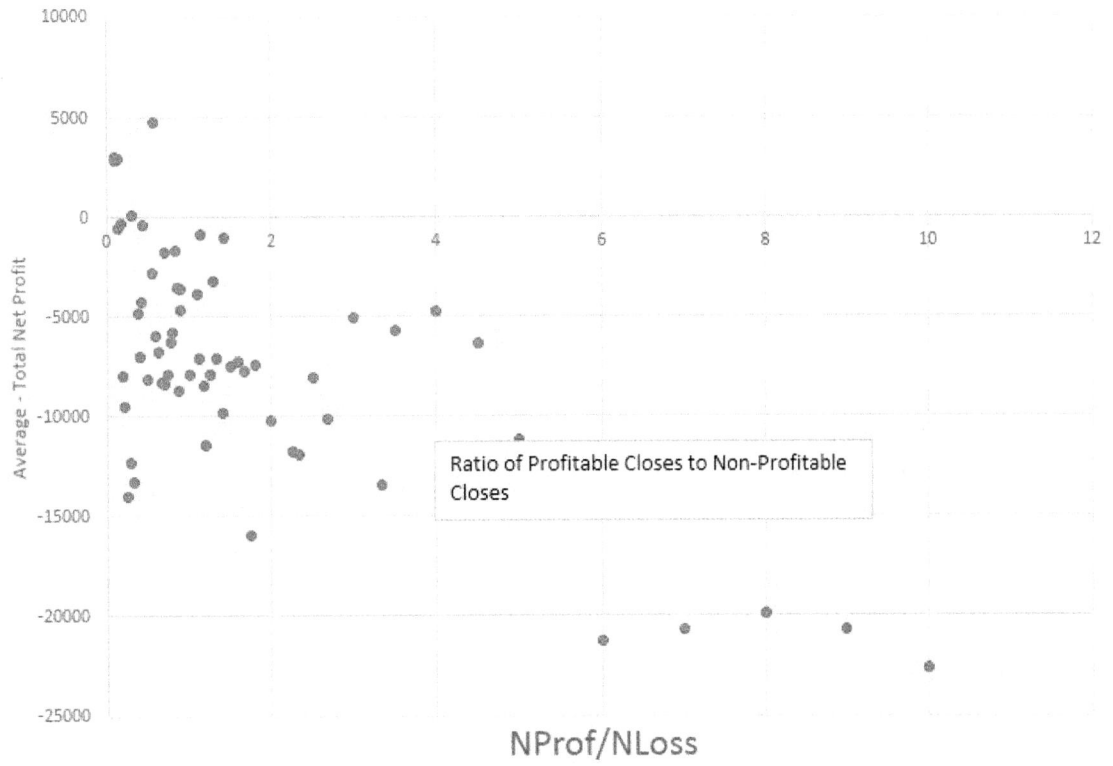

ES - Avg Total Net Profit With Commissions and Slippage

Ratio of Profitable Closes to Non-Profitable Closes

NProf/NLoss

ES - NProf Bars With S&C

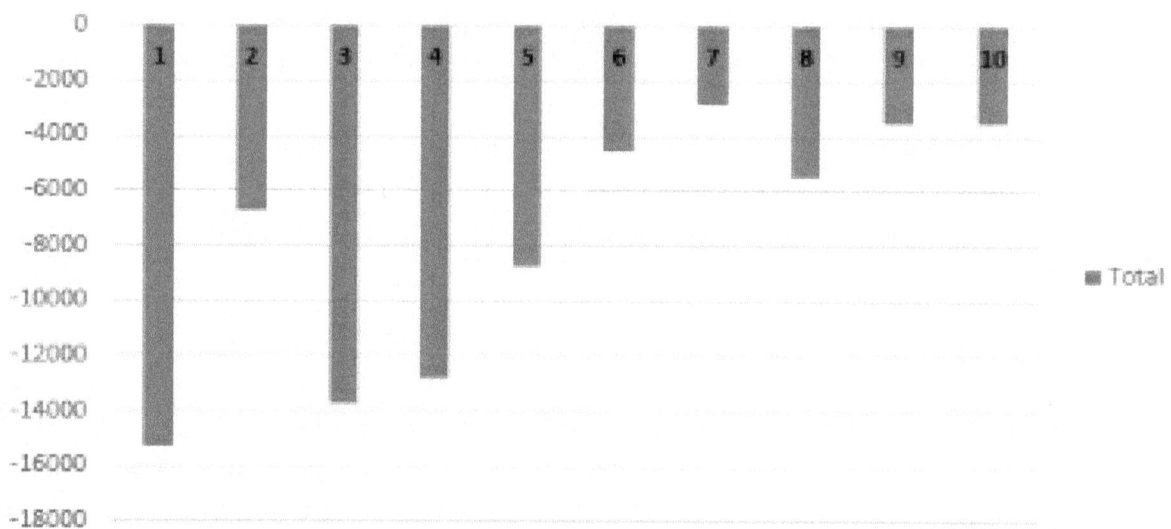

ES - NLoss Bars With S&C

Figure 88- Mini S&P- NProf/NLoss Results

The results for gold show a peak around 2.0 for the NProf/NLoss ratio. This means ideally you'd like to exit at every 2 profitable closes for every 1 profitable loss. But when you break down the results purely by NProf or NLoss, a value of NProf=9 is best, along with an NLoss of 1.

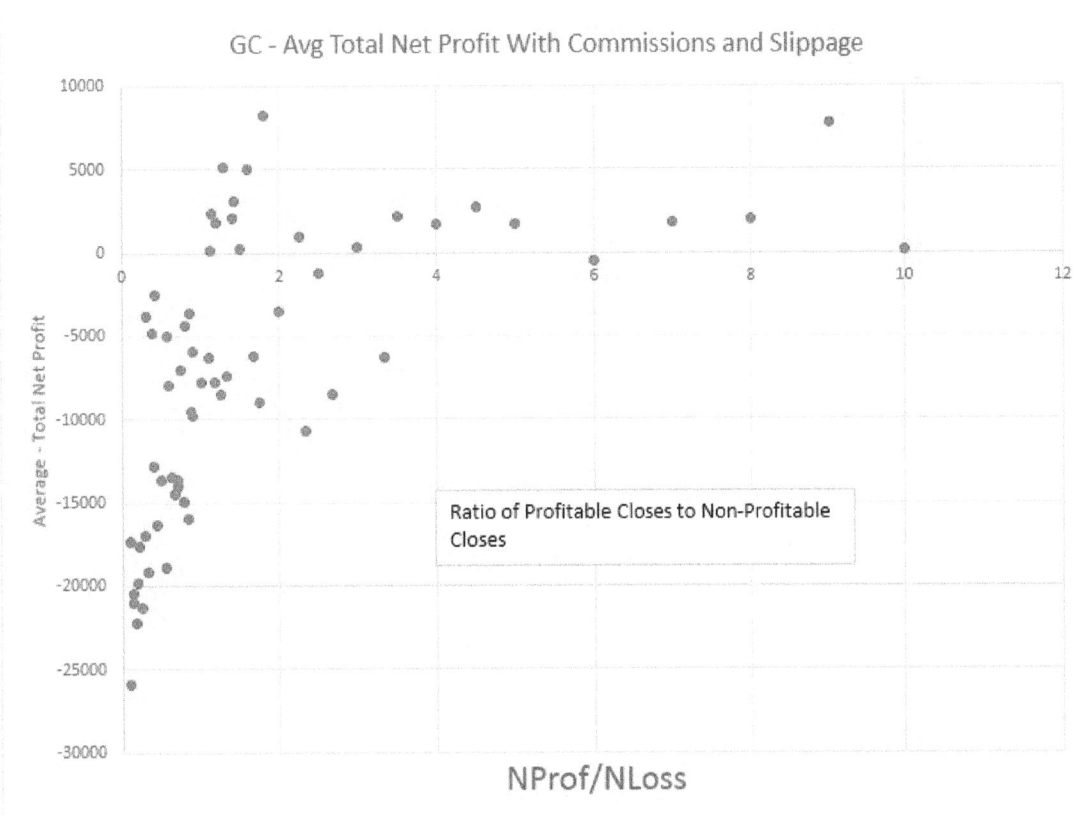

GC - Avg Total Net Profit With Commissions and Slippage

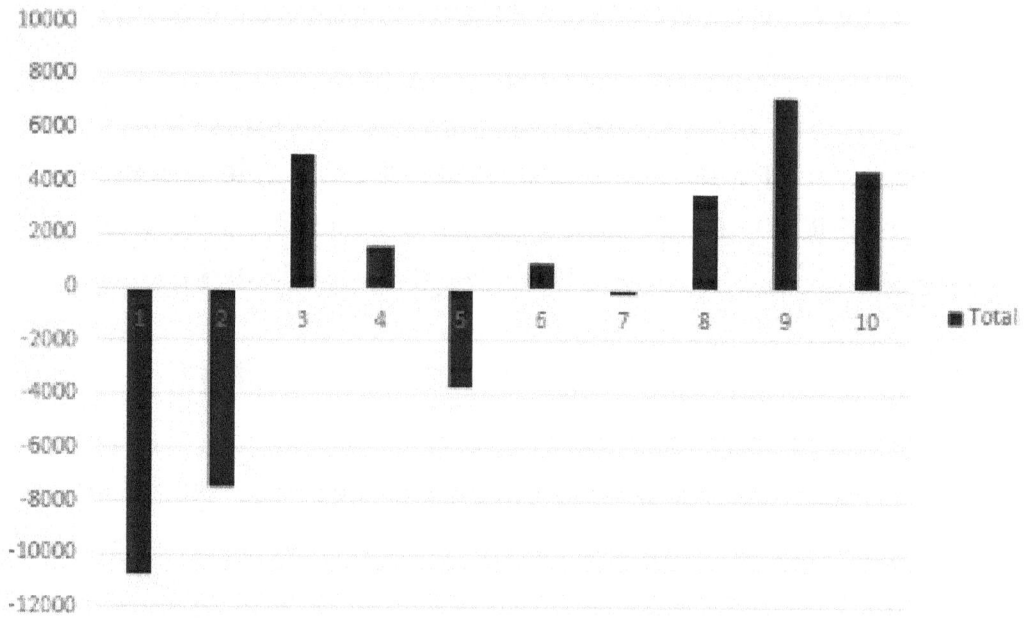

GC - NProf Bars

GC - NLoss Bars

Figure 89- Gold- NProf/NLoss Results

No matter what you do with 10 Year Treasury notes (TY), it will not be profitable. The best results – still negative – are when NProf is small, and NLoss is large.

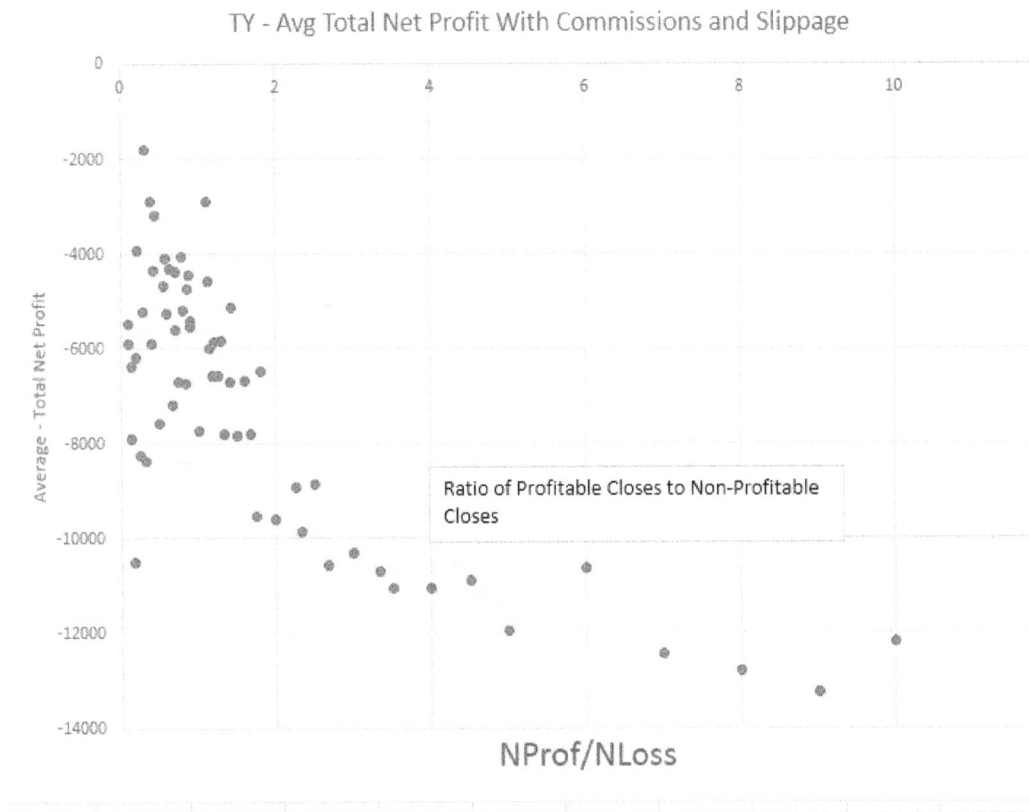

TY - Avg Total Net Profit With Commissions and Slippage

Ratio of Profitable Closes to Non-Profitable Closes

NProf/NLoss

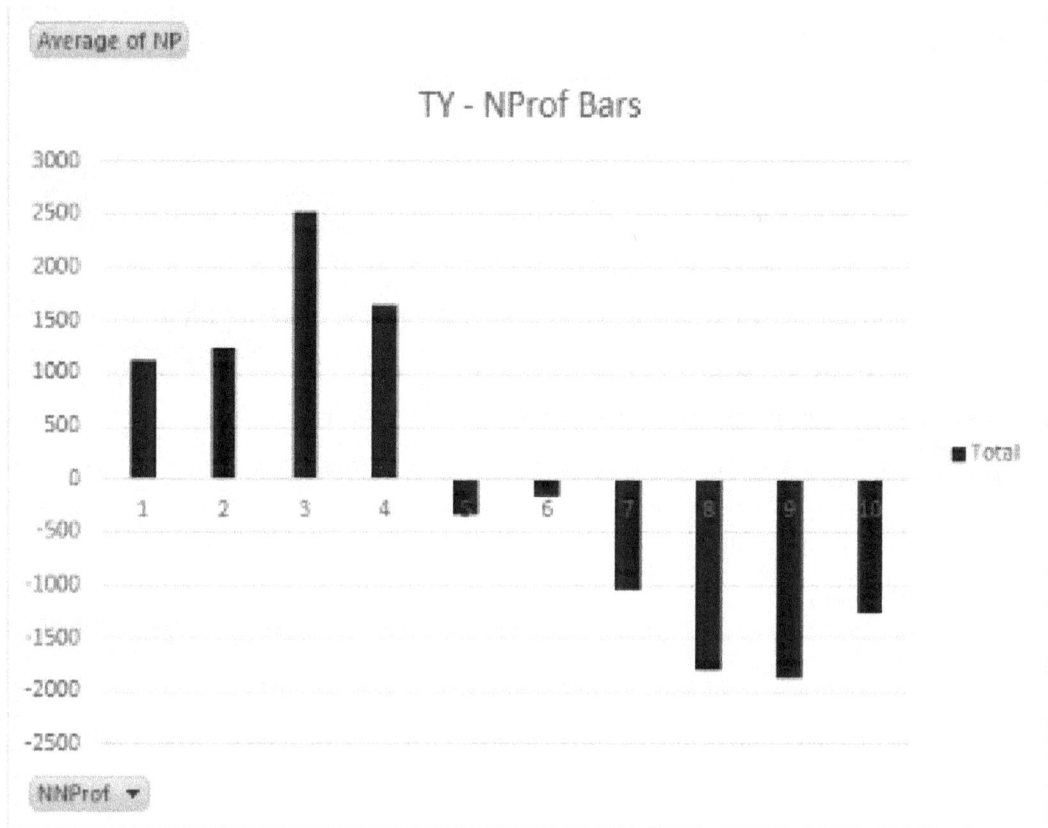

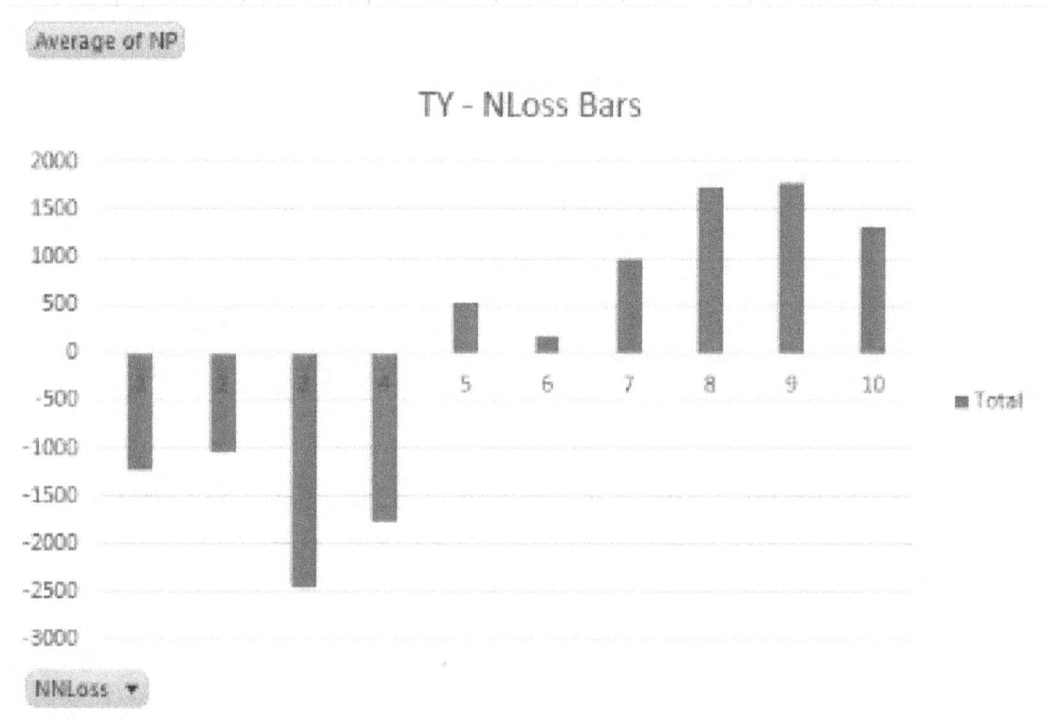

Figure 90 - 10 Year Treasury Notes- NProf/NLoss Results

Cotton and Euro Currency results look similar to TY, except a bit more profitable (and sometimes even net profitable overall). Again, a small number of profitable closes relative to losing closes works best.

CT - Avg Total Net Profit With Commissions and Slippage

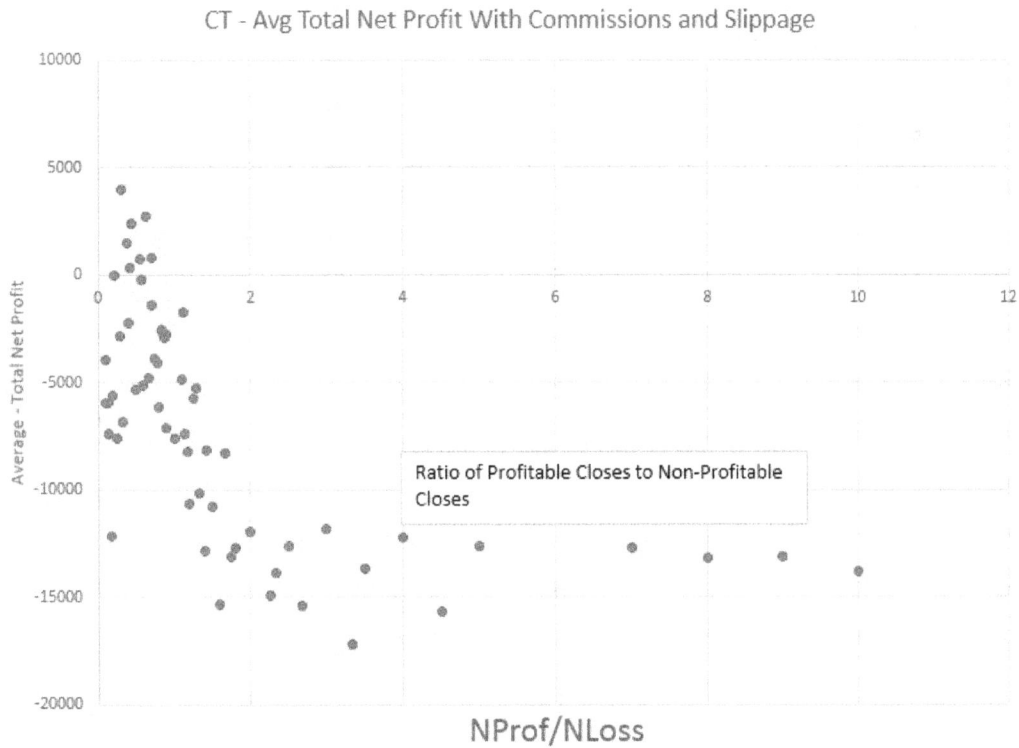

Ratio of Profitable Closes to Non-Profitable Closes

NProf/NLoss

CT - NProf Bars With S&C

CT - NLoss Bars With S&C

Figure 91- Cotton- NProf/NLoss Results

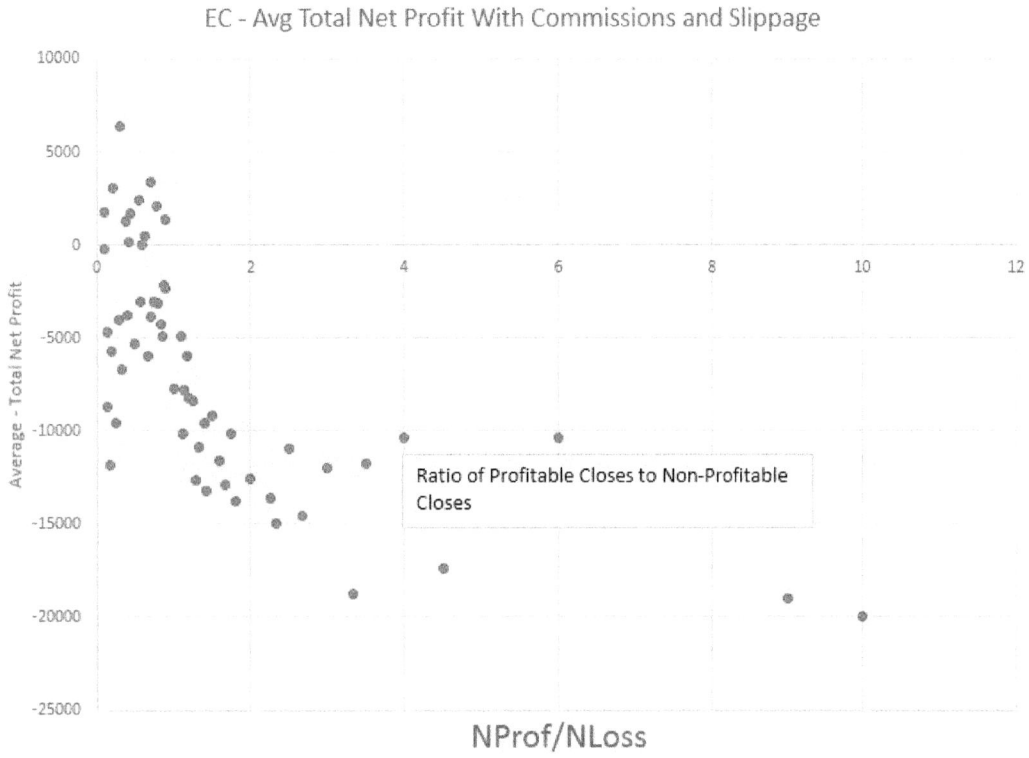

EC - Avg Total Net Profit With Commissions and Slippage

Ratio of Profitable Closes to Non-Profitable Closes

NProf/NLoss

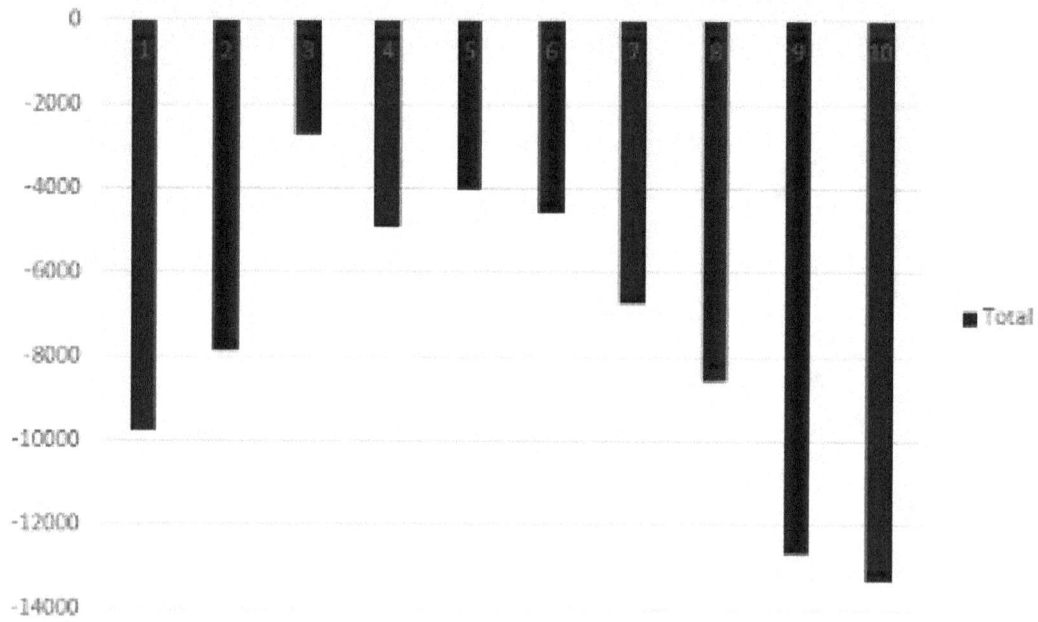

EC - NProf Bars With S&C

EC - NLoss Bars With S&C

Figure 92 - Euro Currency- NProf/NLoss Results

The final 2 markets I looked at – Soybeans and Crude Oil – tend to favor larger profitable closes and smaller losing closes. This is especially true for Crude Oil.

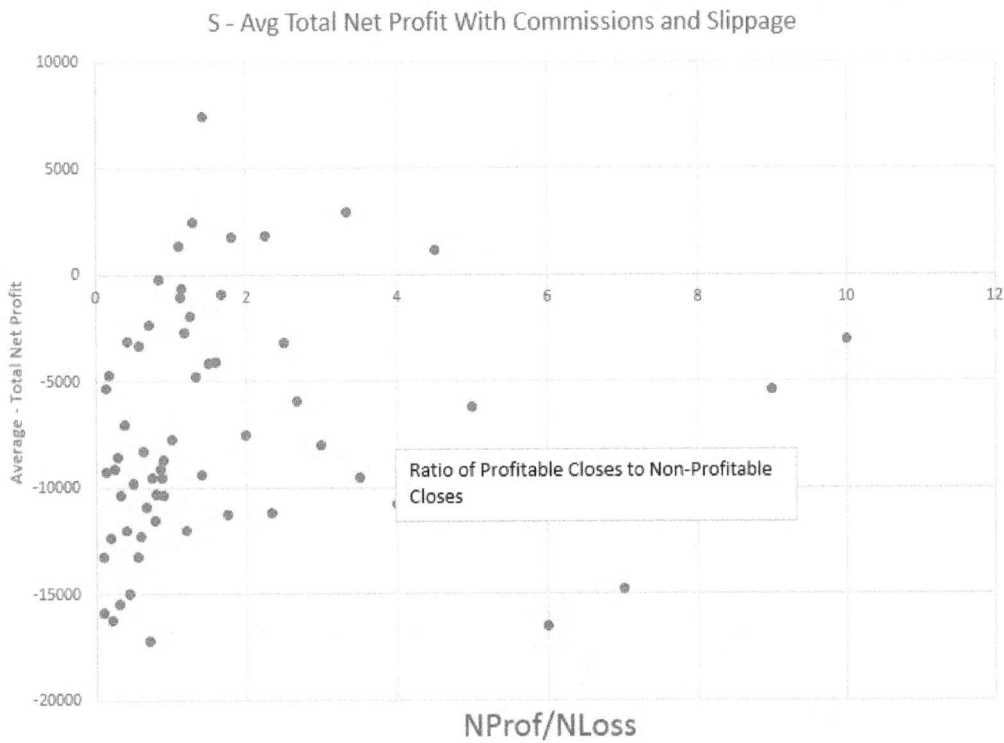

S - Avg Total Net Profit With Commissions and Slippage

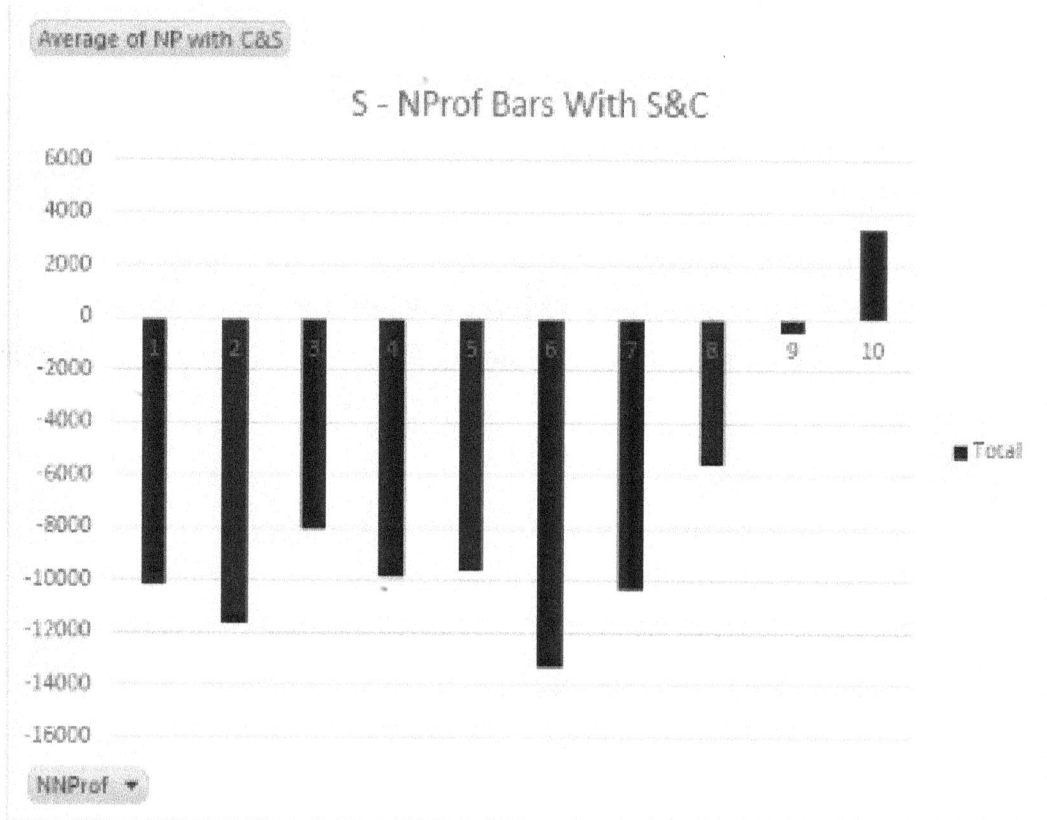

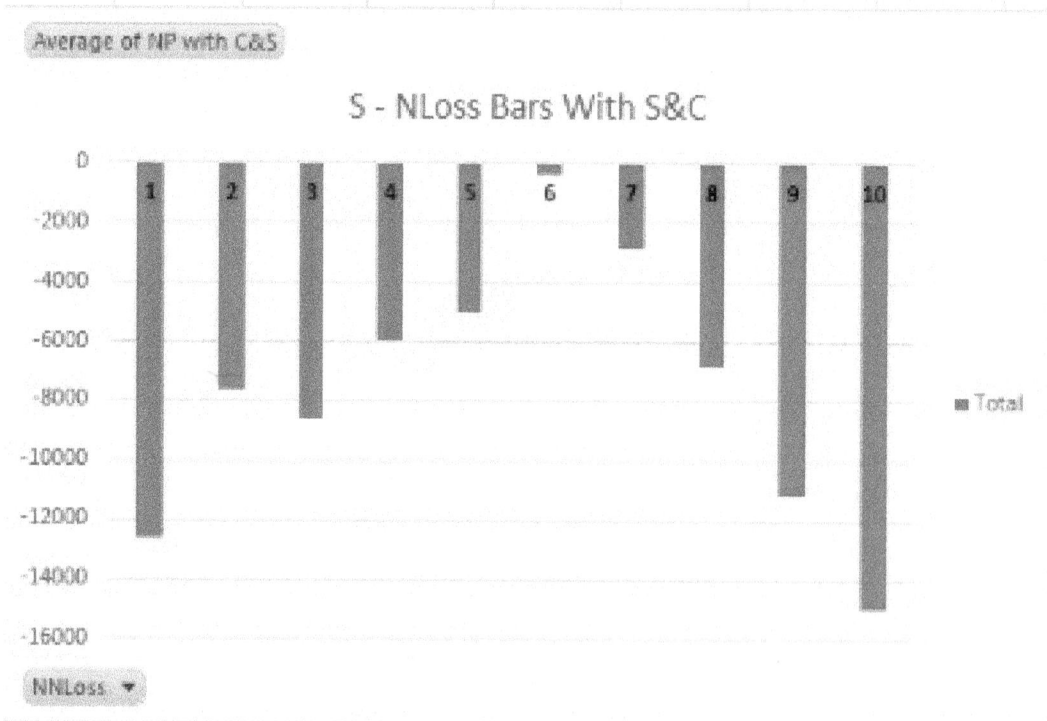

Figure 93 - Soybeans- NProf/NLoss Results

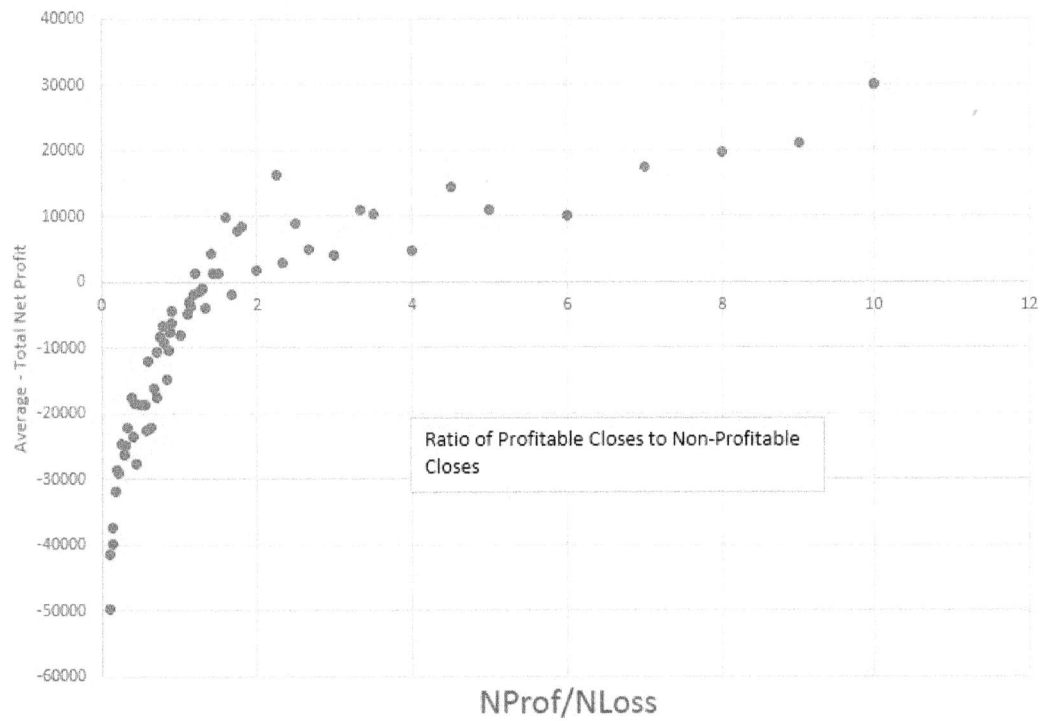

CL - Avg Total Net Profit With Commissions and Slippage

Ratio of Profitable Closes to Non-Profitable Closes

NProf/NLoss

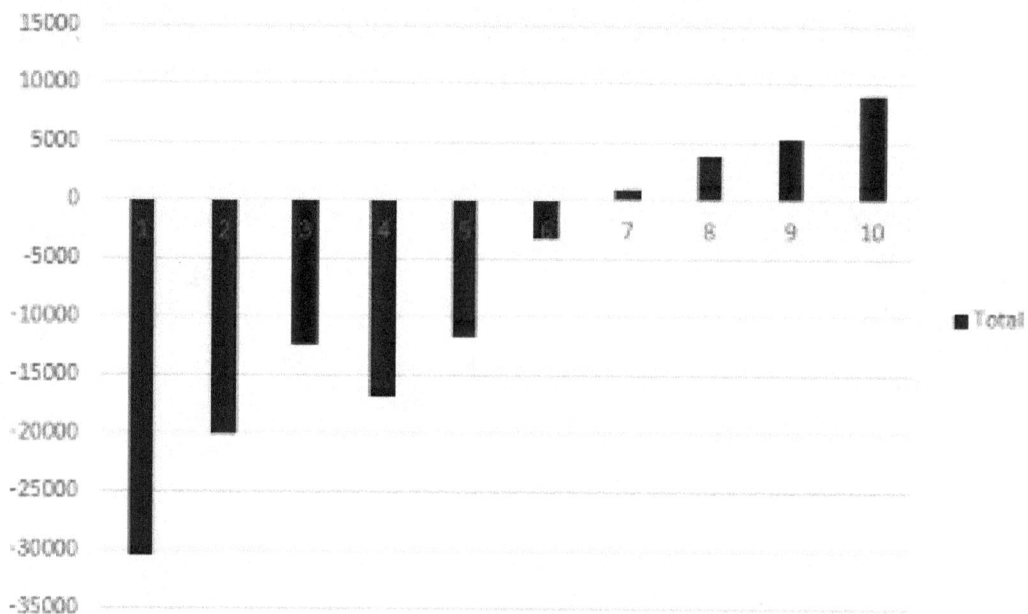

CL - NProf Bars With S&C

CL - NLoss Bars With S&C

Figure 94 - Crude Oil - NProf/NLoss Results

Results - Summary

Looking at the table below, it is clear for most markets a small value for NProfitable closes is best, along with a large number of NLoss closes. But for Gold, Crude Oil and Soybeans, the opposite is true; big profits with small losses are the best.

Market	Best NProf/NLoss Ratio	Best NProf	Best NLoss	Chance Win with Best NProf NLoss
ES	0.57	4 (loser)	7 loser	53.3%
GC	1.8	9	1	54.8%
TY	0.3	3 loser	9 loser	44.2%
CT	0.3	5 loser	10 loser	53.3%
EC	0.3	3 loser	10	57.3%
S	1.43	10	6	61.5%
CL	10	10	1	72.5%

Algo Trading Cheat Codes

* There is no universal optimum N profitable closes exit, no optimum N losing closes exit, and certainly no ideal ratio of the two

* If you want to use this profitable close or non-profitable close approach in your strategy, consider running a random entry study like I did first, to help you decide how to set the proper values

* One thing I did not investigate here is the "NProfitable closes" exit by itself, which is what Larry Williams initially did. Perhaps the NProfitable closes approach, along with a stop loss or even a stop and reverse, would produce good results

* Except for CL, this strategy is not profitable with random entries. It is

interesting that for CL over 70% of the cases with NProf=10 and NLoss=1 are profitable. Let winners run and cut losses short seems to work best for Crude Oil, but not other markets

CONCLUSION

Algo trading is tough, without a doubt. But so are other types of trading. Algorithmic trading has a lot of dead ends, and most of the time the strategy developer wastes time chasing down fruitless ideas.

Utilizing some or all of the Algo Trading Cheat Codes I have detailed here, the strategy creator can save a lot of time by concentrating on the best ideas and concepts.

Here is a handy list of all 57 Cheat Codes:

Chapter 1 - Is Algo Trading Getting Harder?
* Use a strategy development process that has been proven to work in real time, with real money
* Try to be unique in your strategies, bar sizes, etc.
* Don't rest of your laurels – continuously improve your trading
* Expect strategies to eventually stop working, and be prepared with new strategies ready to take their place

Chapter 2 - Full Time Algo Trading
* Realize that the dream of full time trading is much different from the reality
* Make sure you are profitable on a part time basis before attempting to trade full time
* Consider outside trading related activities (signal providing, for

example) to smooth out your personal net worth and income equity curve

Chapter 3 - General Algo Trading Tips
* Consider using strategies without stops, if you can handle the psychological stress
* Don't expect a strategy to work in every market
* Test multiple bar sizes
* Always include slippage and commission costs
* Testing is more than just optimizing - make sure you test enough to properly evaluate a strategy
* Even a good strategy development process does not guarantee success
* Don't forget about risk. Don't focus on just profits
* More optimizing is usually not better
* Patterns and general observations are only building blocks in a strategy. They are not final strategies
* Always perform out of sample testing (I use walkforward testing)
* Millions of iterations do not lead to better real time performance
* Good algo traders use indicators, patterns and other techniques that are profitable in test
* Exits are usually an afterthought, but they are vitally important to good algo trading
* Psychology is more important to algo trading than you might think
* Nothing is trading is guaranteed

Chapter 4 - Bar Size Study
* Slippage and Commissions can be a killer factor for smaller bar size strategies
* If you want to run smaller bar sizes, more focus should be on reducing trading costs. There are really 2 ways to do this:
1. Use limit orders where possible (just realize they have drawbacks in backtest and live trading, especially with "touch fills")
2. Trade less! This study was "always in" – a better approach with small bar sizes would be to have a strategy that was much more selective about taking trades

* Breakout strategies with larger bar sizes can be profitable even after slippage and commissions. They may not be that appealing, though, on a risk adjusted basis

* As always, use my research as a starting point for your own work. For example, if I was to look for a new strategy to develop, I would first focus on larger bar sizes such as 1440 minute bars

Chapter 5 - Mean Reversion Study

* Mean Reversion techniques can be a great way to diversify your strategies

* Best approaches using a single Mean Reversion technique:

2 – Short Term Connors RSI

3 – Bollinger Band Stretch

4 – Moving Average Stretch (best overall)

6 – N Consecutive Bars Up/Down

7 – Reverse Breakout

* Mean Reversion techniques are more powerful when "stacked" together - just watch out for too few trades

Strategy 2 AND Strategy 3 AND Strategy 4

Strategy 2 AND Strategy 3 AND Strategy 4 AND Strategy 7

Strategy 2 AND Strategy 4 AND Strategy 7

Strategy 2 AND Strategy 4

Strategy 2 AND Strategy 3 AND Strategy 4 AND Strategy 6 AND Strategy 7

* Combining Mean Reversion techniques in an either/or setup does not improve overall performance

* Timed exits (at least for exits after 7 bars) makes Mean Reversion performance worse

* "Quick" exits using Mean Reversion decrease performance

* On an overall scale, rates, stocks and energies perform the best with Mean Reversion

* Ags/Softs by far are the worst for Mean Reversion

* As always: test everything yourself to verify

Chapter 6 - Risk Protection Techniques

* 4 unique ideas can reduce the risk of an algo trading system:

1. Daily Loss Limiter
2. Entry Delay After Losing Trade
3. No Weekend Positions
4. High Volatility "Kill" Switch

* These 4 ideas can be used alone, or together, depending on your objectives

* Don't expect them to improve profit performance, but they may help improve your risk adjusted performance

* These techniques will help you psychologically, and that alone might make them worth doing

* If you want to add these to your strategy, remember:

A. Incorporate technique in the strategy, before testing (don't add these to already developed systems, since you'll likely only accept them if they improve performance, which is a form of optimizing)

B. Make sure to properly test and build the strategy (the Strategy Factory process is ideal for this)

C. Optimize these as little as possible. Try to select parameter values you feel comfortable with, rather than picking the best result from optimizing

Chapter 7 - Bull/Bear Regime Trading

* Momentum with flat periods and volatility/volume filter #8 works best for regime trading

* Momentum buy/bear filter only is second best choice

* Trend Based Bull/Bear/Flat Regime filters on average improve net profit, and reduce drawdown

* Volume and Volatility based filters can improve results

* As with all filters, it is advised to add the filters to your strategy BEFORE you do full testing

Chapter 8 - Exit Testing

* When Developing a Strategy, First Try Stop & Reverse Exits, Before Adding in Time Based Exits

* In most situations, the best exit is a simple Stop & Reverse, compared to simple stop losses and profit targets. Profit targets by themselves would be the next best option

* Breakeven stops are almost as good as Stop & Reverse

* Technically Based Exits – Exits that are independent of the entry or the current position profit/loss, are worth testing

Chapter 9 - Reward To Risk Study

* There is no universal optimum Reward to Risk ratio

* If you use profit targets and stop losses in your strategy, consider running a random entry study like this first, to help you decide how to set the Reward:Risk

* If you test very small profit targets and stop losses – where both could be hit on the same bar – make sure you use Look Inside Bar Backtesting or Bar Magnifier, depending on your software. Otherwise your results could be incorrect

* This study shows you MIGHT be able to make money trading a random entry strategy! Look at the table above, the far right column. It says if you ran a random entry strategy with a 2.0 PT and 7.0 ATR, you'd actually have a 89.4% chance of ending up with a profit! I don't necessarily recommend it, but it is food for thought…

Chapter 10 - Profitable Closes Study

* There is no universal optimum N profitable closes exit, no optimum N losing closes exit, and certainly no ideal ratio of the two

* If you want to use this profitable close or non-profitable close approach in your strategy, consider running a random entry study like I did first, to help you decide how to set the proper values

* One thing I did not investigate here is the "NProfitable closes" exit by itself, which is what Larry Williams initially did. Perhaps the NProfitable closes approach, along with a stop loss or even a stop and reverse, would produce good results

* Except for CL, this strategy is not profitable with random entries. It is interesting that for CL over 70% of the cases with NProf=10 and NLoss=1

are profitable. Let winners run and cut losses short seems to work best for Crude Oil, but not other markets

I use these Cheat Codes in my own strategy development, and I hope you decide to also. You can avoid a lot of non-productive testing by using these codes. That will help make you a faster and more efficient strategy builder.

Good Luck!

www.ingramcontent.com/pod-product-compliance
Lightning Source LLC
Chambersburg PA
CBHW081811200326
41597CB00023B/4227